House Beautiful

SMALL SPACE LIVING

House Beautiful

SMALL SPACE LIVING

Susy Smith

EBURY PRESS
LONDON

First published in 1993 in Great Britain by Ebury Press
an imprint of Random House UK Ltd
Random House
20 Vauxhall Bridge Road
London SW1V 2SA

by arrangement with National Magazines plc

British Library Cataloguing-in-Publication Data

A catalogue record for this book is available from the British Library.

ISBN 0 09 177555 8

EDITED BY Emma Callery
DESIGNED BY Terry Jeavons
ILLUSTRATIONS by Ian Phillips Dip. Arch. RIBA

TYPESET by Textype Typesetters, Cambridge
PRINTED AND BOUND in Great Britain by Butler & Tanner Ltd, Frome &
London

Contents

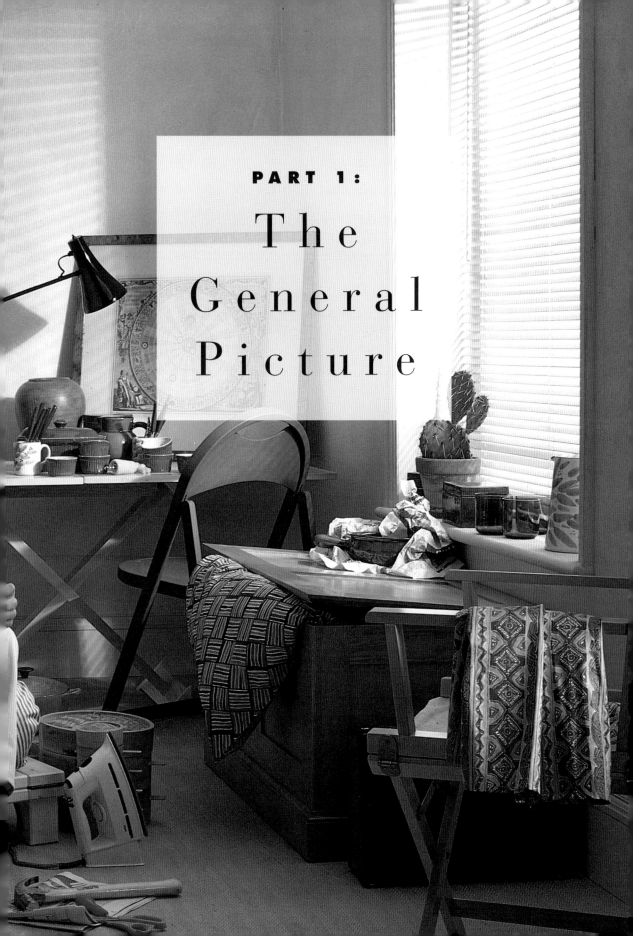

PART 1:

The General Picture

Making the most of what you have

However much we love our homes, we almost always wish them bigger. We could always do with that one extra bedroom, a slightly larger sitting room or a less miniscule bathroom. Well, here is proof that not only are there ways to extend your home, there are also endless ideas you can use to make it appear bigger too.

When you first walk into a home several things will strike you. You may be attracted by a colour scheme, you might be intrigued by the owner's possessions or your eye may be caught by a view through a window. But one of the first impressions you will get, although it may initially be a subconscious one, is of its atmosphere.

You may immediately think how light and airy it feels. Conversely, you may find it dreary and depressing. This impression is created by a number of elements — the size and layout of the rooms, their architectural detail, the colours they are painted, the style and arrangement of the furniture and last, but not least, the lighting.

The way in which these elements work individually and also how they combine make the difference between a pleasing and an uncomfortable interior. So when we talk about the best use of space we are referring to the impression of space as well as actually creating more room to move.

Structural changes

Unless you can afford to move somewhere larger, the ideal way to get the extra room you need is, of course, to extend your home. You may think that the only way to do this is to have an extension built, but if you can't afford such a thing, there are ways of extending which don't have to involve major structural work.

A GARDEN ROOM

Garden rooms (or conservatories) are all the rage these days, and we're not just talking about the reproduction Victorian types which can cost a great deal of money. At most large garden centres you will see a display of modular, aluminium-framed conservatories which, though they may

Treat your garden as another room when weather permits. Here, floral curtains frame the view beyond and provide a taster of what's to come.

not be as pretty, are considerably cheaper than a custom-built conservatory.

Whatever you choose will depend on your budget, but, if you have a garden and are prepared to lose some of it, then adding a 'garden room' is a great way of gaining extra indoor space which will be unlike any other room in your home. The light in a room largely constructed with glass is a new experience for most of us, and people who have a conservatory say that they would never now be without one. The fact that the room opens out onto a garden too is an instant attraction and has the effect of bringing the garden indoors. The other advantage of a conservatory over a brick extension is that you often won't need planning permission for it, although it is advisable to check this out with your local planning officer.

Even if you don't have a garden, you can still have a conservatory. Specialist firms can design them to sit on top of an existing extension at the back of the house, to fit in the gap which often runs between two terraced houses, or indeed almost anywhere there is enough room. We are talking quite a lot of money here though, but if you can't afford to move, or don't want to, then it's worth calling a few specialist firms in to look at the site and get their opinion — and quotation.

MORE ROOM AT THE TOP

Another way to make more space is to move up rather than out. The structure of your house and when it was built will dictate whether or not a loft conversion is a feasible option. If you are going to do anything more involved than boarding over existing joists to use your loft for storage, then it's wise to consult a structural engineer for advice or call in a specialist company who will handle everything from drawing up the plans and installation to liaising with planning officers.

The cost of the job will depend on what you want. For example, a permanent staircase is much more costly (and difficult to site) than a folding ladder; swing and tilt windows, are simpler to install than dormer windows, and so on. But what your investment will give you is a lot of extra space — often enough for a bedroom and en-suite bathroom or shower room, a playroom or, if you need it, office space for working from home.

If you don't have the budget, or indeed the space, to extend your living area, don't despair — there are ways of adapting what you've got. And this brings us on to layout.

Ingenious planning has provided an extra sleeping area in this small flat. Wasted space on the high ceilinged landing was used to extend the staircase and install a small gallery.

Layout

Making good use of our space is something that we all do instinctively to some degree. At the very least we arrange our furniture so that we can move about the room freely.

A dream bedroom for a lucky teenager. Floor space provides a work area, sofa and storage, while a ladder leads up to the bed on a platform built in the corner of the room.

And we try to keep our homes tidy, knowing that a room which is cluttered or untidy is rarely a restful environment to be in. But in the smaller home it is necessary to be a little more inventive about how we allocate our space.

GALLERIES

For instance, if you are short on floor space but your rooms have high ceilings, how about expanding upwards? Galleried rooms are not only the preserve of stately homes. In a bedroom, the bed can be placed on a raised platform with either a small staircase or even a ladder to reach it. This is an idea which will delight children of all ages — it has an air of the treehouse about it! It is a job which can be done by the competent DIY fanatic although you may need to seek advice from a professional structural engineer on weight and structural implications. Otherwise there are companies which specialize in this type of work who will give you a quotation.

FLOORS

A room arranged on more than one level will always look more interesting than one on the flat. If you don't feel you can run to a galleried room, how about simply raising part of the floor? This works best in a larger room, but we have also seen it used to stunning effect in the 3×3.5m(10×12ft) front room of a Victorian terraced house. A raised area helps to delineate between, say, a dining and sitting area; or in a bedroom, it can provide the ideal site for an en-suite corner bath. The step up can be as little as 30cms(12ins), and instantly, you have the feel of another room within a room. Again, you will probably need to seek expert advice

A rounded archway delineates living from sleeping space in this top floor studio flat. The unusual kitchen units have been custom-made to suit the style and shape of the flat.

for this type of work to get the load-bearing specifications correct. But once that is done this is a job which you could carry out for yourself.

STAIRCASES

Staircases take up a lot of room because of their shape and in most homes leave space underneath which is rarely put to good use. There are two solutions here. Spiral staircases are a pleasing shape — indeed, they often become a feature of a room, and occupy much less space than their straight-as-a-die counterparts. You can buy them pre-cast in metal or could have one custom-made in wood. Aside from fitting into a corner of a room, the spiral shape has the effect of leading the eye upwards — instantly you know that there is something else to see, psychologically giving a feeling of more space.

If you prefer to stick with a straight flight of stairs, you have two options. In the 1960s and 1970s it was very popular to install open-tread staircases. Rather than being faced with the solidity of a closed-tread flight of steps, open-tread stairs help to create a feeling of space because you can see through the gaps. Such a staircase can, however, look rather dated these days, unless in a very hi-tech environment. The best solution really, is to make the most of the space underneath. Instead of remaining a dumping ground for old tins of paint, the kids' discarded toys or the pile of newspapers waiting to go for re-cycling, this space, strange shape though it may be, can be put to good use.

The obvious application is as an extra loo. This prevents queues from forming outside the bathroom during the morning rush and will also add value to your house, if and when you come to sell. There are many small cloakroom washbasins on the market which will fit neatly into a corner and the old fashioned WC with a high cistern is back in vogue and saves on space.

Another thought is to install a shower. If the space isn't large enough for a separate cubicle, then the whole room can be tiled from top to bottom to become a walk-in shower room — a real luxury.

Whether you go for the loo or shower room, you will need to seek expert plumbing advice to check that water supplies can be connected, that the water pressure is sufficient for a shower and that the loo can be connected to the main soil stack. It's best to call in a reputable firm — or someone who has been recommended — to carry out this type of conversion from start to finish. Then if you have any problems, you have some comeback and they should return to sort it out.

Depending on the amount of space under your stairs, you can apply it to suit your needs. If it is really tiny then you may only be able to use it as a cupboard for coats. If it is a fair size and has a window, it could become an area for the kids to do their homework or for you to have a small desk where you can do your paperwork or write letters in peace. It could be a place for the freezer if you can't fit it in your run of kitchen units. Or, again if plumbing is possible, a small utility area for washing machine and tumble-dryer, or even just somewhere to stack the ironing until you get around to doing it.

CHIMNEY BREASTS

Many homes which lost their fireplaces with the fervour of central-heating installations in the 1950s and 1960s will have chimney breasts which were bricked up and plastered and now sit as blank walls, hiding usable space.

The fashion now, happily, is for fireplaces to be reinstated, but this is not always suitable or possible. You can, however, still open up this space and put it to other good use. In the kitchen, it provides the ideal site for a cooker — particularly in a country-style kitchen where you may be installing an Aga or other cooker which is attractive as well as functional. Alternatively, a fireplace would offer ample space for enough wine racks for even the most discerning of wine buffs.

Proof that no space need be wasted, this chimney breast in a well-planned kitchen has a dresser built into it. There is room for display, storage and even a small wine rack.

In the sitting room or bedroom, shelves could be built into the space to store books or display favourite possessions.

Organizing the furniture

Quite aside from utilizing wasted space in the ways we have already described, a little extra thought on the actual layout of your furniture will also play its part in giving you more room to move.

The small sitting room in this Victorian terraced house is well laid out. The original fireplace is one focal point, another is the marble-topped table in the bay window. The disparate pieces of furniture are unified by a centrally placed rug which also brings colour and pattern to the room.

When devising the layout of a room, the aim is to create an arrangement which is not only practical but also visually pleasing. We do this almost instinctively; placing our prized pieces in prominent positions, pushing less attractive objects into corners, balancing a large piece of furniture against one wall with something which matches its stature on another. But while we are doing this we should bear in mind the function of the room.

In some cases this will require much pre-planning — in a bathroom or kitchen particularly. Here we cannot move the furniture around when we tire of the layout. Our requirements must be thought out before the furniture is fixed and fitted, and with luck, what we end up with, is a room where the space is made the most of and it functions well to suit our individual requirements.

When planning a bedroom or sitting room, it helps to think along the same lines. What will you use the room for most? Which pieces of furniture will you need to fill it? Once you have decided on the main elements, think about how you can make them work for you. Where possible, pieces of furniture should serve a dual purpose or be adaptable — tables which fold out, chairs which fold up, shelves which are adjustable to different heights.

WORKING AROUND A FOCAL POINT

The starting point for any room, whatever its function, should be a focal point. This is exactly as it sounds — an element which is the main attraction; a central pivot around which everything else radiates. In the bedroom it will usually be the bed; in the bathroom — the bath; in the dining room or kitchen — a table. In the sitting room? Well this more variable — it might be a large sofa. It might, heaven help us, be the television. Or it might, as it always was in the past, be a fireplace.

It's interesting to note that all those fireplaces which were ripped out for the 'Contemporary' look in the 1950s, are fast finding their way back into blank chimney breasts.

A handsome pine fireplace is very definitely the main focal point in this living room. A matching overmantel mirror both reflects the stained glass motifs at the window and brings extra light into the room.

And that even many modern homes, built without chimney breasts, are proudly sporting non-functional fireplaces against flat walls. Fashion dictates aside, many homeowners are realizing that a fireplace gives a sitting room its central point of focus. So unless you intend to use your chimney breast for one of our storage ideas mentioned earlier — put a fireplace in. This will give you something to work your scheme around.

Once you've found you focal point, you can work the other pieces in around it — but do stop before it becomes overcrowded. In a small room, try to keep the centre of the room free. Admittedly, when all the furniture in a room is placed around the edges it can look a bit like the setting for a barn dance, but a centrally placed rug which meets the individual items of furniture will anchor them and hold the arrangement together.

Think of ways of using redundant areas such as alcoves or bay windows more inventively than simply hiding them behind a sofa. For example, you could build in a bench with storage underneath.

Where there are cupboards, think about having the doors hinged in the middle as well as at the sides. Then they can double back on themselves when open, like shutters, and so won't catch on pieces of furniture near to them.

continued . . .

strategically placed large mirror, you will be amazed by the amount of extra light it brings to a room. And not only that, its reflections fool the eye into believing there is more to see than is really the case.

One of the best places to use a mirror is at the end of a long, dark hallway. It will pick up the light from the front door or any windows and will throw light back into gloomy areas. Position it facing a window in a sitting room or bedroom and the reflection will fill the area with brightness. It will also duplicate the colours and shapes from its surroundings and if these are light and bright, so much the better. Incidentally, this is also a favourite ploy with garden designers for magnifying a modest plot. A length of mirror placed on the wall at the end of a garden, preferably under an ivy-covered arch, will fool the casual observer into thinking there is much more beyond.

● **The garden** *If you've got one, it pays to treat it as another room. At best, you will have doors from a sitting room opening onto this extra space, which you can expand into for at least a few months of the year. Or at the very least, you have it as a view.*

LIVING DAYLIGHT

Here are three practical styling points for you to consider, to help create effective lighting arrangements in your home:

● *Vary the positions. Bright, evenly lit rooms quickly become stressful, so create pools of light in different areas of the room at different heights by using a combination of uplighters, table lamps and wall fixed lights.*

● *Exploit texture. Without shadow, texture can't be revealed and the overall feel of the room becomes two-dimensional and uninteresting. Shadows are produced only when the light is directional, so the angle is crucial.*

● *Use dimmers. Dimming switches are an easy way to create variable moods within a space to suit changing needs at different times.*

Six different light sources are at work here, illustrating how effective a combination of lighting types can be. Aside from the picture light, wall washers and table lamps which are immediately visable, an uplighter is concealed behind the plants, a spotlight (out of shot) highlights the coffee table, two recessed ceiling spots light the area by the window.

Lighting

We have left lighting till the end, not because it is the least important of all our ideas, but because it can only play its part some of the time, because of course its effect is irrelevant during the day. It is, however, one of the easiest and most effective ways of changing the atmosphere in a room.

Think of a room where the only light sources are two or three table lamps. The shades will soften and sometimes colour the light and the effect will be one of several pools of warm light illuminating selected areas. The parts of the room which are not furnished with one of these lamps will be in shadow — so the room will look cosy.

Add to these a couple of wall lights — uplighters, which direct their beams onto a ceiling which is painted a light colour. The light will bounce back from the ceiling, so giving an overall feeling of brightness.

These examples illustrate the way in which light can change the whole look, feel and mood of a room. The very best solution for lighting any room is to have a mixture of sources. Lighting specialists abhor central ceiling pendants, because the light they give is so indiscriminate and bland, but most of us are stuck with them so the ideal option is to supplement them with other lighting such as table lamps or wall lamps.

In an ideal world, all the sources will be wired onto a circuit with a dimmer facility. Then we can turn the lights down low for a quiet night by the telly, or lift the mood and size of the room by having them on full brightness.

So, you see, there are many ways to make small homes feel bigger. But remember that we all want our homes to feel comfortable, warm and inviting and this is often much more difficult in a larger home. The rooms can be too large and the ceilings too high to ever create a feeling of cosiness. So if you're finding your current surroundings a bit cramped, look on the bright side — a smaller house can feel more intimate, is easier to heat, and cheaper to decorate.

COLOURS AND PATTERNS

Forming the backdrop

Colour is the single most influential element we have at our disposal for use in the home. A colour change can transform the same room from warm to cold or large to small. It can give a feeling of well-being or it can be oppressive. Pattern and texture too play their part. It is by manipulating these valuable elements that we can create a pleasing and spacious environment.

The most obvious solution when decorating a small room is to paint it white to compensate for the lack of space. White, with its reflective qualities, will bring light and air to the most cramped interior.

However, white walls are also very harsh. When the room is full of sun, the effect can be almost blinding, and on a dull day, the room will seem grey and bleak. So while white may be the obvious choice, it is not necessarily the best one. Besides which, you can have fun playing with more imaginative options such as off-white or cream. These do the same job as white, but because they have a little yellow in them, will also bring some warmth to the room.

However, even choosing cream can be a bit too safe. Many people are frightened of using colour in their homes, in case they make an expensive mistake. As a result, Britain is full of houses with magnolia walls which neither make a statement nor create a very interesting environment. In this chapter we hope to convince you that colour is not difficult to use if you follow a few basic ground rules. More specifically, we'll also show you how colour and pattern can be used to your advantage when decorating the smaller home.

The psychology of colour

Beyond the practical considerations, most of us rarely think further about why we have actually selected particular colours for our interiors. The most obvious reason is because, presumably, we like them. But the intriguing question is why?

One reason is because of their associations. Yellow, for example, is a sunny colour. It's bright and it's cheerful and so is most often selected for kitchens or breakfast rooms and for children's rooms. We associate blue with water, so it's a favourite choice for bathrooms. Pale pinks and peaches are

Inventive use of colour can bring a whole new dimension to an interior. Here a fresh and vivid green is the backdrop for crisp white, dark mahogany and touches of gilt.

soft colours and so we often feel the only place we can really get away with them is in the bedroom. Greens are an obvious choice for a conservatory or garden room.

On another level we are also subconsciously making a statement about ourselves — psychologists claim they can tell a lot about the homeowner's personality from the way in which he or she chooses to decorate. Inevitably, people who choose bright or strong colours are generally considered to be much more outgoing and extrovert than those who select the safer colours.

More importantly, those in a quandary about whether their sitting room should be green or blue should remember that psychologists also believe that colour has a marked effect on our moods and how we feel after spending any time in a particular room. Blues, for example, are generally

WARM vs COOL COLOURS

WARM COLOURS
Yellow
Orange
Rust
Red
Pink
Purple:
is the cross-over point. A purple with a lot of red in it eg burgundy or maroon, is warmer than a regal, true purple. And as this purple changes to violet, so it begins to move towards the cooler end of the spectrum.

COOL COLOURS
Violet
Blue
Aqua
Turquoise
Emerald
Lime green
is the changing point — as greens move through into yellow, they become more vibrant and become warmer colours.

considered to be restful and calming. Spend more than a little time in a room with walls painted in a strong yellow or red, however, and you will probably feel quite unsettled and ill at ease. Dark purple or chocolate brown will create a heavy, oppressive atmosphere, where the walls and ceiling seem to be bearing in on us and make the room feel claustrophobic.

While there is probably some truth in all this theory, it can really only apply to extremes, for if we dilute any of these strong colours the effect will differ. A gentle pink or soft primrose yellow will make a room feel warm and restful. Swap purple for lilac or chocolate for a milky brown and the whole atmosphere changes to something which is much easier to live with. So however many rules are written, it is difficult to generalize about colours as each one has so many different shades and intensities. There are, however, several more down-to-earth methods of deciding on what will be the correct colour choice for your situation.

What is the function of the room?

What you actually use a room for, and how often, should be a major factor in deciding your choice of colour. If it is a family room then practicality must prevail — pale coloured sofas and cream carpets do not mix with muddy feet and sticky fingers. If you are decorating a bedroom, then you can afford to be a little more self-indulgent and plump for softer shades which might seem out of place downstairs.

The time of day when the room is most often in use should also be taken into account. In a formal dining room or a sitting room which is mostly used at night, colours can be rich and dark to give a cosy feeling, whereas brighter, lighter shades are more in keeping for a breakfast room or kitchen. A bedroom can really be either — a light, bright, fresh colour-scheme will give you the impetus to get up in the morning, or you can go for something much more dark and decadent.

Creams and lemons are a
good choice to keep this
kitchen/breakfast room as
light as possible. A sliding
door combats the problem
of limited space and leaves
room for a pine chest of
drawers in the alcove.

How much natural light does it get?

Another aspect to take into account before you decorate is the direction your room faces. This will dictate how much, and what kind of, natural light comes into the room. And, of course, the size of your windows will also be a contributing factor. Assuming you want the room to have as much natural light as possible, you may have to create a balance with the colour you decorate it.

If your window faces north, and therefore receives little or no sunlight, you may want to compensate for the lack of sunlight by choosing a 'warm' colour. If you face south or west you will get lots of sunlight and the room may actually become too hot in the summer. In this case, you might want to cool it down by selecting a 'colder' colour (see the panel on page 26).

The two situations we have given are the most extreme examples — yours may not be so cut and dried. But basically, it is important to stand back and assess the room you are about to decorate. Once you can see what kind of light is in it at various points through the day, you will be able to decide whether or not it is necessary to use colour as a compensatory factor for too much or too little existing light; experiment a little.

Visual trickery

When you are decorating a small room, the size is an important factor to take into account. There are several ways in which you can use colour — and pattern too — in order to trick the eye into believing that a room really is bigger than it actually is.

Deceiving the eye is surprisingly easy. The French phrase for the technique — 'trompe l'oeil' ('deception of the eye') — perfectly describes the way tricks can be played in interiors to fool the observer into believing something which is not quite what it seems. At one end of the scale are marvellous murals painted to depict scenes like a window

A mid to dark colour will give a ceiling more emphasis — thus making it seem lower and the room less lofty. To give a chimney breast and fireplace more prominence, paint the alcoves either side in a contrasting colour.

Adding a dado rail with different colours above and below will create extra interest in a room but also has the effect of visually dividing it. This is a good ploy in an over large, chilly room but can work against you in a small room.

Paler colours create a lighter — and larger looking — room. If you do add a dado, keep the colours above and below it to similar tones. This makes it seem larger. Decorating a room in varying shades of the same colour is always a good formula for success.

overlooking rolling English countryside, where in fact the other side of the wall is a gas works; or an Italinanate courtyard wreathed in bougainvillea on the wall of a two-up, two-down in Watford. There are many specialist designers and artists who can create one of these scenes for you — or if you feel up to it, you could even have a go yourself.

Less grand, but equally effective, are the simple ways in which we can use plain colours and patterned wallpapers to fool the casual observer.

Using colour

As we mentioned in the first chapter, colours can be divided into two groups — retreating and advancing. These do exactly the job their names suggest. When used on walls they either have the visual effect of making walls seem to move away, so making a room seem bigger, or they appear to bring the walls inward — making a room seem smaller.

The colours are differentiated simply by their intensity — pale colours, particularly from the cool end of the spectrum, are retreating colours, and dark or strong shades or those from the warmer-end of the spectrum are advancing colours. To illustrate the point, here are two extreme examples. A room with rust-red walls will feel warm — think back to our colour associations of red as a 'hot' colour — and because this is an intense colour the walls will seem much closer, making the room seem smaller. In contrast, think of a room painted in a pale blue. Blue is a fresh, cool colour and because it is used here in a diluted form, the room will seem more open — and larger.

So if we apply all our rules to a small bedroom which faces north and doesn't get much natural light, then we could choose to decorate with a pale pink or pale yellow which would solve all the problems in one go. Pastel shades are an obvious choice for bedrooms. Either of these colours will warm up a north-facing room, and because the shades are pale they will make the walls recede and the room seem as big as possible.

If you want to solve the opposite problem and bring a wall visually closer — perhaps at the end of a long hallway or narrow galley kitchen, a strong, advancing colour will do the trick. By bringing the end wall towards you, the room also seems to be wider.

This trickery doesn't work only on walls. You can make a low ceiling seem high by painting it a light colour or bring a high ceiling downwards by using a darker tone than on the walls.

In the smaller home, continuity of colour is the key to success. This doesn't mean painting every room the same colour, but rather creating a flow throughout the home. You could, for example, keep the carpet the same throughout the ground floor and continue it up onto stairs and landings. You can still vary the colours used on walls, but the floor will provide a unifying factor.

Using pattern and texture

Pattern and texture play a part in every room however plain and simple, and we can use both to create differing feels for our interiors. When you are working with a small space

There is quite a lot of pattern in this tiny bathroom but it works because of a common colour theme of pale blue and white. Furniture and picture frames in rich browns are strategically placed for symmetry and balance.

PAINT FINISHES

Always start with a small wall to gain confidence and complete one whole wall in a session — you will see changes in the pattern otherwise.

EMULSION GLAZE is simply made from emulsion paint with water added. A good ratio is 550ml water to one litre of emulsion paint. Only apply this glaze over walls painted with matt emulsion.

OIL GLAZE Mix:

- *One part of coloured eggshell paint*
- *Two parts of oil glaze*
- *Quarter pint of white spirit.*

Oil glaze dries slowly so you can wipe off mistakes with a little white spirit on a rag. It can only be applied on top of eggshell or vinyl silk paint and when dry should be protected with two coats of matt or eggshell lacquer.

SPONGING

- *Use a natural sponge for a better variation of texture.*
- *Wet the sponge with water and squeeze it out well to expand it back to its full size.*
- *Dip the sponge into the paint and then blot onto a spare piece of scrap paper to distribute the glaze evenly over the sponge and to prevent runs and blobs in the pattern.*

which you want to make larger, the simpler the pattern the better. A wallpaper with a busy pattern for example, is the wrong choice.

WALLS

Introducing interesting textures rather than large patterns on wallpaper work to your advantage as they add interest without being predominant. This is one of the reasons why woodchip wallpaper became so popular in the 1970s. When painted with a plain colour it added texture to walls and proved a little more interesting than a flat surface. There are, however, more up-to-date alternatives. Self-patterned wallpapers and fabrics for example, retain a continuity of colour but introduce the variation of pattern too.

Paint techniques have mushroomed in popularity in recent years for the very reason that they create a more interesting and varied effect than plain walls without becoming a dominating factor in the room. Such paint techniques as sponging and ragging give a broken surface effect. They always look their best when executed using two tones of the same colour rather than a mix of colours.

Vertical stripes are a classic pattern which work well in almost any setting and have the added advantage of making a ceiling seem higher. These can either be on wallpaper or you can paint them onto lining paper using low-tack masking tape to delineate the edge of the stripes.

FLOORS

When you are choosing flooring there are many options other than carpet and some of them such as sisal and wood veneer will introduce subtle and interesting textures and have a natural charm too.

WINDOWS

Pattern can be introduced at windows in many ways other than the obvious one of choosing a patterned fabric for curtains. Etched glass is an unusual and effective choice

continued . . .

● *Hold the sponge at arm's length and dab it gently onto the wall.*

● *Dot the sponge about so that the marks you make are more random and natural.*

● *Don't aim to cover all the base coat with your sponging — some of the base colour should always show through.*

RAGGING

● *Different fabrics give different effects so experiment— cottons, chamois leather and even plastic bags are all good materials.*

● *To start, bunch up the rag in the palm of your hand and dip into the paint.*

● *Blot off excess paint by dabbing the rag onto scrap paper. This will also indicate how your pattern will look on the wall.*

● *Lightly press the rag onto the wall surface, turning your hand and rebunching the rag from time to time so there's lots of variety of pattern. Change your rags whenever they get clogged with paint.*

particularly where you want to let light in but retain privacy. It comes in many different designs and will cast patterns onto the wall too.

Patterned sheers and voiles play the same part as net curtains in the home, but look much more unusual. Some designs are self-coloured, others include colour as part of their pattern, and all have a wonderful filigree effect as the light shines through them.

So even if you don't have the budget — or the space — to make major changes in your home, experimenting with colour and texture can be fun and is one way to overcome the problems of living in compact surroundings.

ABOVE: Patterned glass introduces subtle textures to interiors and often adds another dimension by the way in which the light is filtered and diffused.

Putting your house in order

You can never find things when you want them . . . When you open the cupboard under the stairs, everything falls on top of you . . . You never have enough shelf or cupboard space anyway. Know the feeling? Read on. We tell you how to put your house in order, squeezing the proverbial quart into a pint pot.

However well organized they are, most homes never have enough storage space. The advent of the completely fitted kitchen showed us how cleverly, well-designed storage can cater for our needs, often within a limited space. Realizing the potential and popularity of custom-designed storage, manufacturers have now moved on — to the fitted bedroom and bathroom. If you are starting to furnish your home from scratch and can afford it, it's worth getting estimates from reputable companies to see what they can offer, they may have the answer to all your problems. If not, don't despair, there are plenty of quick and easy ways to utilize your space more wisely without spending a fortune.

The first consideration is to identify exactly what it is you need to store. In the modern home this can range from linen, to books, to children's toys. Next you need to look at how you can use any available or wasted space to its best advantage. An obvious area to exploit (unless you happen to live in a bungalow) is the space under the stairs. In every room there will be items you want to keep on display and those you would rather keep hidden behind closed doors, so in most cases you will want a combination of storage which allows you to fulfil both these criteria.

Shelving need not be purely utilitarian. Depending on how you stock your shelves, they can become a feature of a room — but you do need to keep them tidy.

The living/dining room

The items most likely to need consideration here are books, magazines and ornaments which you will want to keep out either for display or easy access. In addition, there will also always be other paraphernalia you would rather keep hidden. So the best plan is to have a combination of cupboards and open shelving.

Shelving is not just a convenient and easy method of storage. It can often add its own decorative element or even become the focal point of an interior. It can be used in much the same way as a picture frame, surrounding favourite and treasured possessions and showing them off to their best advantage.

Floor standing shelving units have the advantage that you can position them where they will be most useful and can take them with you when you move. The designs at the upper end of the market are often well designed too, giving you a mix of shelves for display, sometimes with undershelf lighting; deep cupboards with shelving to store items such as CDs, LPs or cassettes; a pull-down flap revealing a drinks area, and so on. These usually come as part of a modular system where you can select the elements which best suit your requirements and they will match up together. It is best to choose as varied a combination as possible, for example mixing a couple of glazed top units with shelves and solid base units. Perhaps choose an end unit which is slightly lower in height, and if possible continue the run round a corner onto the next wall. In this way, you will have a substantial number of units and plenty of variation. The most uninspiring sight in any room is a run of solid and blank cupboard doors.

The much simpler and less expensive choice is an open shelving unit perhaps in a light wood such as ash or beech, with a little individual detailing such as cross struts at the back. These units are a good discipline for those inclined to be untidy as there is nowhere to hide anything! The drawback with floorstanding shelving units is that they often end up occupying valuable wall space where you might want

Alcoves can be put to good use either for built-in shelving, cupboards, or, as shown here, for a storage seat. Once the hinged top is down, a foam cushion is placed on top to provide a comfortable extra seat — ideal when you're short on space.

to site a radiator or place a sofa. The alternative, building your own shelving, is relatively easy and it can be custom designed to fit into limited or awkward spaces which would otherwise be redundant. You can either buy the components as part of a shelving system and install them to suit your individual requirements or if you are fairly competent at DIY, you can build your own system. If you are buying from a ready-made system, it's best to make sure you choose uprights which allow you to adjust the height of each shelf — in this way you can move them to accommodate different heights of books.

The kitchen

Kitchens these days are much better organized areas in terms of saving space than they used to be. But this is through necessity as much as choice. Although the kitchen is heralded as the hub of the home, where the whole family congregates, by and large, kitchens are getting smaller. So we, and the makers of kitchen units, have to be ever more inventive.

If you can afford a fitted kitchen, then much of the hard work is done for you. You simply have to tell the designer your requirements and wait for the whole thing to materialize. But if you are stuck with someone else's kitchen which doesn't suit you or if you can't afford to shell out for a fitted kitchen then you need ways to make the most of what you've got.

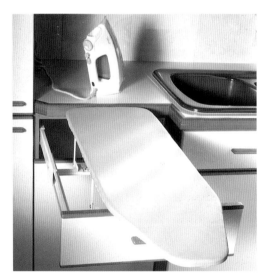

A brilliant concept — an ironing board which unfolds from a drawer should put paid to all your washday blues.

For a start, a tidy kitchen always looks bigger, so keep your work surfaces as clutter-free as possible, just bringing out appliances such as food mixers and toasters when you are actually using them. To store as much as possible away, you should fit extra shelves inside units. If it's a base unit, you can remove the shelf completely and replace it with a set of wire baskets on runners to pull out easily. These are great for keeping pans and their lids tidy, and mean you can get right to the items at the back of a cupboard without having to lift everything else out first. Choose a combination of shallow and deep baskets to suit the items to be stored.

Corner units in kitchens are notorious space wasters, so fit a carousel unit in place of a shelf. Or attach a shaped wire shelf to the door which swings out when the door is opened, allowing you access to all the items on the shelf.

One place where space is almost always wasted in fitted kitchens is under the units, where a plinth panel is put in to hide the gap between the floor and the base of the unit. A few manufacturers are now realizing that even this space can be put to good use, and are installing under-unit drawers as part of some ranges.

Baskets or plastic boxes on runners are often more practical than shelves. You can get right to items at the back and cuboards are easier to keep clean.

Large DIY stores stock a range of kitchen accessories to fit standard base and wall units. These include various internal fittings for cupboards and drawers including different sized wire baskets.

For expanses of wall where there are no cupboards, you could fit a simple wire grid with 'S'-shaped butcher's-style hooks to hold cups, mugs and utensils, or even use a piece of expanding trellis from the garden centre, cut to size, to do the same job. In fact, when you are short on space it makes sense to hang what you can on walls or even on the ceiling. There are now circular hanging racks for ceilings and straight hanging bars for walls which will hang pans and utensils, making them easy to reach when you are working but avoiding these bulky items taking up vital cupboard or drawer space.

The bedroom

Storing clothes is the priority here, but making room can be a nightmare with cupboards bursting at the seams and drawers full to overflowing. If there is no room for extra storage furniture, you need to organize the space inside wardrobes and drawers to make the best use of it.

The simplest solution for untidy drawers is to buy dividers. These are inexpensive lengths of perforated plastic which you can snap apart to fit each drawer. They act rather like a cutlery tray in a kitchen drawer, dividing it into neat partitions each of which will hold an item of clothing such as a pair of socks or knickers.

To make use of the 'dead' areas in wardrobes, double your storage space by fitting a second hanging rail halfway down the wardrobe for shorter items like jackets and skirts. You can buy a plastic hanging bar very cheaply to hook onto your existing rail. And to prove that manufacturers are ever mindful of just how common the problem of finding enough storage

Out of season clothes and spare bedlinen can be stored away neatly, but kept to hand should you need them, in these specially designed storage boxes.

really is, they have come up with many more clever ideas to help us solve it.

Shoe tidies come in a variety of sizes and help you avoid a desperate scramble to retrieve the other one of a pair of shoes from the bottom of the wardrobe. These hook onto the door or sit in the base of the wardrobe. Ties, scarves and tights all become creased, jumbled and impossible to sort out if you keep them in drawers. the solution to this problem is a hanger with several clips or holes which will keep your fashion accessories in perfect order. If you don't even have the space for a wardrobe, a hanging rail of the type used in clothes shops might suffice. You can buy fold-up nylon 'shelves' which clip onto it for jumpers and to keep the whole lot concealed, a folding screen pulled across will do this trick and look decorative too.

Sorting out-of-season clothes is always a problem. Pack

Make the most of the storage space you've got with good organization. This combination of hanging rail and baskets for jumpers, shoes, etc, is a good all-round solution for the chaotic wardrobe.

them away in the loft and you can bet your life that June will bring an October-like day and you will end up rummaging around in a dusty suitcase, trying to retrieve something warmer than all the summer cottons you have kept in the wardrobe. One solution is to pack them into a blanket box or ottoman placed at the foot of the bed. At least access is then easy and you can use the top of the chest for a tea tray and books or magazines as well.

The other obvious place is under the bed, but this is a prime dust-gathering area, so your clothes should be packed into a well-sealed box or case. You can now buy attractive containers designed specifically for this purpose. Made from soft plastic in a variety of designs from very smart stripes to pretty florals, they are large enough to hold a number of jumpers and blouses, and if you pack them properly, should remain sufficiently uncreased to be taken out and worn again when winter comes around. The manufacturers of plastic storage boxes for food have also scaled up their models to make them large enough to pack clothes or linen in. They have an airtight seal to prevent dust from getting into the contents.

For dresses and coats which are better kept unfolded, you may prefer to buy a temporary wardrobe. Again available in a number of different patterns of soft vinyl, these act rather like a suit bag, although they hold a fair number of hangers and can be folded flat and stored away once you no longer need them.

If you're about to buy a new bed, choose one with storage drawers fitted underneath which will also give you room to store items of clothing without taking up more and possibly limited wall space.

You can create storage in the most unexpected of spaces. The room above might look like a study, but look a little closer and you'll see that what appears to be a desk is, in fact, a bath.

POSITIONING SHELVES

The obvious place to site shelving is in an alcove, but look at corners too. With a little extra thought and planning, shelves made to fit into alcoves can be designed to continue round a corner onto the facing wall. This will give you more storage space and a more interesting shape.

This wall space above windows is rarely used for anything else, so if you are building shelves, consider continuing them around and above a door or window. This not only increases your potential storage space but also attractively frames the window and its view, making the whole arrangement a focal point in what might be an otherwise architecturally uninteresting room. A display shelf running round a room at picture rail height is another idea for under-used wall space. It will provide somewhere to keep books or china and looks decorative at the same time.

If you prefer a less 'fitted' look for your living space then you are more likely to choose individual pieces of furniture to fulfil your storage needs. In this case, try to find items which offer storage but double up for another purpose too. Seating such as upholstered stools or blanket boxes can also give you valuable storage space inside. Side tables and coffee tables with shelving or cupboards underneath will perform the same function. A sideboard or dresser, either in old pine or a more contemporary style will give you display space on top with plenty of shelves and cupboards below. And a corner cupboard is another piece of furniture which combines the decorative with the practical and is ideal for the smaller sitting room or even in otherwise wasted space in a hall or stairway landing.

The main thing to remember before you buy any large pieces of furniture is to measure up and take a tape measure with you so that you can choose sizes and shapes to suit your space.

TECHNOLOGY GOES TINY

Essential items for small spaces

Technological wizardry has transformed the modern home, saving us all time and effort in the process. The real bonus for those with limited space is that virtually any labour-saving appliances or gadgets you can think of, from cookers to computers, come in scaled-down versions.

The domestic environment of the 1990s would be barely recognizable to our great-grandparents if they were suddenly transported through time into a modern-day sitting room or kitchen. Jobs which 50 years ago were done by hand or with limited mechanical aid, are now almost entirely carried out by machines which, in a lot of cases, we simply programme and then leave to get on with it.

A vast choice of electrical gadgetry is there for the taking. Having decided on the jobs we want them to do, all that remains is to find the model which suits our pocket, style and situation. It is, of course, the third point which particularly concerns us in this context. It's all very well knowing you need a fridge, a cooker, and perhaps a washing machine, tumble dryer and/or dishwasher, but how on earth do you fit them all in? Even the most generous of kitchens will be hard-pushed to accommodate all the appliances which we have come to take for granted as the essentials of modern day living.

Then there is the sitting room, too. Whether you can afford them or not, can you actually accommodate the television, the video, the stereo system and maybe even the computer without your room beginning to look like the electrical floor in a department store?

Well, the great thing about technology is that it is ever developing. In order to tempt us to throw away the old and invest in the new, manufacturers are constantly seeking ways in which to upgrade and improve their wares. One aspect of this endless development is that the workings get smaller and smaller so space can be found, in even the tiniest of homes, for at least some of these items. Here we consider cookers, fridges and freezers, washers and dryers, rubbish removal, and the all-important entertainment equipment.

The kitchen

This is the place in the home which has benefitted most from technological advancement. So too, is it the area which requires the most careful planning because, particularly in bedsits, converted flats or modern starter homes, kitchens are often very short of space.

When considering the elements that you want to incorporate in your kitchen, it is important to be realistic.

The 'Micro Kitchen' includes everything the discerning homeowner could want and all in a miniscule space. Fridge, freezer and dishwasher are neatly concealed behind unit fronts, clever wall-rack systems store herbs and utensils, and there is even room for a small TV.

GADGETS

As well as the appliances that play starring roles, we shouldn't forget to mention all the items in the supporting cast which can make your life easier whatever the size of your kitchen.

● Coffee-making is a fine art these days and machines to aid you in your quest for the perfect cappuccino are everywhere. But the occupier of the small kitchen is usually lucky to have room for a kettle and a jar of coffee, never mind a vast chrome machine, hissing and spitting steam everywhere. So to cater specifically for those tight on space, most of the main electrical manufacturers have brought out two- or even one-cup automatic coffee and tea makers which include matching mugs and wall-mounting brackets as part of their design.

● Food processors too come in compact versions, with the smallest models designed solely to chop herbs, nuts and the like and slightly more substantial processors which will cope with anything from egg whipping to coffee grinding, but take up less worktop and cupboard space than their larger counterparts. There are hand blenders too which come complete with a wall bracket.

You should think carefully about what your true needs are and give them priority. It may not be possible to include everything you would like, but with a bit of ingenuity you may be able to come up with alternative ideas. Always plan in advance to ensure that new appliances will not involve you in a total redesign of your kitchen.

Talk to your supplier to make sure that the existing plumbing and electrical sources can be adapted to take your new additions. If there really isn't space to house all the items you need, you could consider using other rooms to house appliances that are not vital for the day to day running of the kitchen. You might be able to keep your freezer or washing machine in the garage, or under the stairs for example.

COOKERS

Unless you are into cooking on an open fire or living on takeaways, you have got to have one. Aside from deciding on whether it should be gas or electric, the other main considerations are how much to spend on it, what will you use it for, and where are you going to site it? Depending on the model you choose, you can have a combination of gas and electricity, two different sized ovens and/or a mix of conventional and microwave functions.

The advent of the fitted kitchen has brought with it the fitted appliance. What is essentially a utilitarian item becomes incorporated neatly into a housing which disguises it. The decision as to how and where it fits in will usually be made for you by the kitchen planner.

If, however, you do not have a fitted kitchen, then allocating the space is down to you. Before you buy, however, take into account how you use a cooker. If cordon bleu cookery is your thing, then your choice of appliance will be a well researched, expertly made and very personal decision. If you regularly entertain or cook for extended family your requirements will be different from the single homeowner or couple who perhaps eat out a lot. But whatever your needs, there are small-scale cookers, just as there are mini dishwashers and fridges which are every bit as efficient as their bigger brothers, and which will fit into even the most cramped of kitchens. For example, the Baby Belling — that basic, cook-it-all machine familiar to bedsit dwellers of the 1960s — has been updated and now comes as a floorstanding model. In addition to two boiling rings, grill unit and oven, you can get a stand which incorporates a pan storage shelf and the whole unit still measures only 39cms (15½ins) high × 46cms (18½ins) wide × 41cms (16½ins) deep.

At the simplest end of the market, there are single and double electric boiling rings which will service quite versatile cooking, so long as your favourite meal of the week isn't the Sunday roast!

Several companies manufacture mini cooking units, which are about the same size as a microwave, and indeed look very similar. They usually provide oven and grill facilities inside the glass-fronted unit and also often have electric rings to make up the hob on the top. A small unit such as this, measuring around 32×57×25cms (13×23×10ins) will take up very little worktop space, or could even be kept out of the way, on a specially built shelf.

The big cooking news of the past ten years has undoubtedly been the microwave. Love it or hate it, the microwave has championed the fad for fast food and become a piece of vital equipment in the no-time-to-cook household. And although most of us choose to combine a microwave with a conventional cooker, there is very little you cannot cook in one of these mini machines, particularly if it combines conventional cooking facilities with its microwave functions. They also take up much less room than a floorstanding cooker.

FRIDGES AND FREEZERS

The fridge is the next vital item for the kitchen — so much so that only about 4 to 5 per cent of households are still

continued . . .

and good length of lead and one of these is all you need to purée fruit or turn vegetables into delicious soups.

● *When the inevitable spills occur, either in the kitchen or on the sitting room carpet, the mini cordless vaccum cleaners come into their own. These must surely be one of the most useful electrical innovations of recent years. Instead of having to get the full size vacuum out every time you knock over a plant pot or spill a packet of cereal, the mini-vac can be unclipped from its re-charger and the mess is cleared up in seconds. These are a great supplement to the standard vacuum cleaner in any household but if you are living in a small home and have stripped wood floors instead of carpet, one of these mini machines may be all you need. They'll get dog hairs off the sofa and fluff out from under the bed, so why shell out for anything larger.*

without one today. Fridges may be fairly innocuous machines which are easy to take for granted, but without them our lives would be much more difficult — ask your grandmother. Doubtless she will remember the changeover from larder to fridge and the wonderful realization that fresh food no longer had to be purchased every day. If you have the budget and the space to add a freezer to your shopping list, then, of course, food storage becomes even less of a problem.

The size of the average fridge usually falls somewhere between 500 and 600mm to fit comfortably with the standard size of the base units in fitted kitchens. However, always mindful of the war on lack of space, manufacturers are now coming up with slimline models which can be up to 10cms (4ins) narrower — precious space in the small kitchen.

Tight corners can be a problem with door swings on cupboards and fridge doors. The best solution here is to install a pull out fridge and freezer. These are designed to be installed as part of a fitted kitchen, with fascias to match the units. They operate like a drawer and contain a sliding shelf storage system with a capacity of around 4ft³. You should, however, check with an experienced kitchen designer before committing yourself to buy, as the expert eye will detect how much space is needed to allow smooth running and to prevent scraping along the sides.

Where floor space is at a premium, one way of getting round the problem is to buy combination appliances — fridge/freezers, washer/dryers and combination microwave ovens. Appliances which stack will also use vertical rather than horizontal space. The ultimate in mini machines are the worktop models which can be placed on a worktop or refrigerator. For example, there is a compact freezer which measures as little as 52cms (20¾ins)high × 59cms (23½ins)

Many modern appliances are available as slimline versions or in miniature to cater for those living in studio flats or the smaller houses of today.

deep. It obviously won't have the capacity to store ready made meals everynight for a family of four, but it is ideal for the studio flat, or as a supplement to a good sized fridge.

WASHERS AND DRYERS

With all the demands placed on your time in today's fast moving world you need all the help you can get. If you don't have the room for a washing machine, don't despair — you don't have to resort to the launderette just yet, and banish the thought of a dishwasher being a luxury. There are washing machines, dishwashers and tumble dryers which are designed to fit in the most unlikely of places.

For a family wash load of clothing you will need a machine of reasonable capacity, but where space is short a combination washer/dryer will at least save you having to find the room for two machines. There are various models on the market which provide the option of wash only, dry only or wash and dry cycle. Try to find a model which doesn't need a venting hose so that the machine can be positioned anywhere.

If there really isn't the space to install any machines in a run of units under the worktop, there are models which sit easily on top of the work surface. One washing machine measures just 45cms (18ins) high when in use (30cms[12ins] when stored) × 45cms (18ins) wide × 40cms (16ins) deep, and it can take a load of up to 2kg (4.4lbs). Features include prewash, soak and main wash cycles as well as a choice of three rinsing cycles and it is also suitable for delicate fabrics. A viewing window and cord storage are also incorporated. An equally small spin dryer can accommodate a load of up to 1.5kg (3.3lbs) and spins clothes dry in just two minutes. It measures 50cms (20ins) high × 35cms (14ins) wide but is best used on the floor rather than on a worktop

A dishwasher might seem an unnecessary waste of space in the small kitchen, but slimline versions like the one below will slot into a narrower gap than normal and still hold a surprising eight place settings.

because of vibration during operation. When thinking about machines such as these, do bear in mind that you will need somewhere to store them when they are not in use.

You may think that a dishwasher is a luxury that small kitchens have to do without, but there are mini models of these appliances too. Guaranteed to take the drudgery out of washing up and neat enough to slide into narrow slots between units or sit on top of standard width worktops, most of these machines will hold six or more place settings. One of the latest models is designed to make use of the space under the sink drainer — a spot which is often under used. Measuring 45.5cms (18ins) wide, it is mounted on a plinth and can be incorporated into existing units so it doesn't have to be fitted as part of a new kitchen.

RUBBISH REMOVAL

Disposal of rubbish is a problem in any kitchen, and is especially annoying when you're short of space. Waste disposal units are one option, but a relatively recent innovation is the trash compactor, which, for the same floor space as a rubbish bin, can deal with a much larger quantity of waste and is eco-friendly into the bargain.

Tiny TVs mean you can tune in even when you're on the move. These models have 6cm (2¼in) screens and integral earphones and aerials.

That's entertainment

Nowhere is small more beautiful than in the field of home entertainment. From personal stereos to pocket televisions, the battle is on to produce the tiniest items which are both portable and stylish.

Whatever you may feel about them, personal stereos are here to stay. Although we usually equate them with noisy youngsters irritating fellow travellers on buses and trains, they are a boon for the household with teenagers when you really cannot stand the thumping baseline from the bedroom stereo any longer. These days you can transport Pavarotti, 'Portugese For Beginners' or your favourite episode of the *Archers* wherever you go in the home or outdoors. Cassette players are still the most popular form of portable sound but are fast being superseded by the portable compact disc player. And when you want to plug into the mains at home you can create a complete sound system with a pair of mini speakers. Measuring around only 10cms (4ins) wide × 12.5cms (5ins) high, they'll fit anywhere you want them. If you confine your consumption of music solely to one room then there are many complete stereo systems with radio, record deck, cassette and CD player all in one unit and these are always getting smaller.

Televisions too come in a wider variety of sizes than ever before. For the smaller home, a 35 or 40-cm (14 or 16-in) screen will fit neatly into most sitting rooms without becoming the main attraction. If you are a real TV freak, these days you can have vision wherever you go. Tiny models with screens measuring just 6cms (2½ins) come with earphones and integral aerials, and a stand should you want to prop them up when cooking the dinner, lying in bed or wallowing in the bath.

Last, but not least, we must include the ubiquitous computer. If you have kids you'll almost certainly have one, and you might even have one of your own — for doing the accounts, writing the best-seller or perhaps for working from home. If this is the case, then the chances are that your office is squashed into a space under the stairs. With more and more businesses being set up on the kitchen table, you're likely to find yourself adding up in the attic or doing the books in the boxroom. Vital office space can be tricky to find — but at least when it comes to kitting it out, microchip technology is on your side. From tiny tape recorders to the smallest computers imaginable, office equipment now comes small scale.

Pocket computers which measure only 20 × 10.5cms (8 × 4ins) are now available which perform several functions from address book and diary with alarm to word processing. To keep it dust free perhaps you should invest in a battery operated miniature vacuum cleaner which comes with a selection of nozzles and has suck and blow functions!

FOLDAWAY FURNITURE

Furnishings with hidden assets

Folding furniture has lost its camp-bed image. Today there are a whole host of clever and stylish designs on the market and most of them are very reasonably priced. So if lack of space is cramping your style, try out these ideas for 'instant' furniture.

The main benefit of folding furniture is its versatility — in seconds a table which displayed nothing more than a fruit bowl and vase of flowers will expand to seat six or eight people; five minutes will turn a comfy sofa into an even comfier double bed, and a flick of the wrist is often all that's required to unfold a few extra chairs when unexpected guests turn up. Pieces of furniture which can perform more than one function are a boon in any home, whatever its size. In the small home, of course, they are vital.

Tables

Few of us need a permanent full-size dining table. It is more likely that the surface will be redundant most of the time, gathering dust and piles of magazines. Better then to select a design which is adaptable, such as the old-fashioned gateleg table or one which has a removable leaf to cater for larger numbers when entertaining, or when feeding the entire clan for Sunday lunch.

Modern versions of these traditional designs are available in light woods such as ash and beech or in a stained finish if you prefer darker woods. Indeed, contemporary designers have come up with a wide range of ingenious tables, designed to suit several situations. There are models where not only the top, but the supports too are hinged, allowing you to transform a narrow console table into a dining table large enough to seat six people. Or what about a dining table for four where both sides flap down when not in use, leaving a top surface the width of a shelf and concealing four matching chairs which are folded up underneath? And you don't get charged extra for this inventiveness — folding furniture is still comparatively cheap when compared to more solid, static pieces.

The ultimate in space-saving dining furniture, this table for four has flaps which fold down when not in use leaving a top surface about 30 cms (12 ins) wide. The matching chairs fold flat and are stored in a cupboard underneath.

You may perceive trestle tables to be the preserve of painters and decorators or church fêtes, but they are, in fact, an easy way of having a dining or work table when you are as short on cash as you are on space. They come in a wide range of colours and sizes — with rectangular or circular tops, in wood or Formica finishes and with legs in wood, coloured metal or chrome. They are incredibly cheap and assembly is easy. Once erected you can leave them as a permanent fixture, or dismantle them after the event until they are required again.

If you lack the space for a separate dining room, or your living room is too cramped for comfort, a wall-mounted table could be the answer. The flap lies down against the wall until you need it, when a hinged strut pulls out to support it. They can be installed in almost any space where there is room to get a couple of chairs up to them — a hallway perhaps, a lobby or small kitchen.

Wall-mounted tables are often the only solution in narrow galley kitchens where they can provide a temporary breakfast bar and then flap neatly out of the way when not in use. They usually have a wipe-clean surface making them ideal for the kids to eat or play at, when you need to keep them under a watchful eye while working in the kitchen. A flap down table can also give you an extra work surface if you are the kind of cook who likes to spread out.

Occasional tables such as coffee and lamp tables in the sitting room should be made to pay their way too. A butler's tray — a wooden tray which lifts off its legs — will give you a small table top for displaying ornaments or better still use it as a drinks table. It can then be harnessed into action when you need to transport coffee and liqueurs to the dining table at the end of a meal, or to take tea out to the garden.

'Nests' of occasional tables are also well worth a mention here. For although most of them don't actually fold, they are designed to fit neatly inside one another and can be pulled out when you need extra serving surfaces. This is a real advantage when you are serving a buffet or an informal family meal. They come in a wide range of styles from mock Tudor to wrought metal.

A great idea for those who love traditional style furnishings and can't bear the blank screen of a non-operational TV staring them in the face, is to hide it behind

There is more to this occasional table than meets the eye. Not only can you use its top to display favourite ornaments and knick knacks, but behind its curtained front you can store your TV, video and cassettes as well.

'curtains'. Sounds ridiculous? Not so! The circular table with its floor-length cloth which has become so popular in recent years is now available as a model which sits innocently in the corner until you want to tune in to your favourite programme. Two hinged arms at the front of the table fold back, taking the cloth with them, on either side of the table to reveal the television underneath. When you switch off, just bring the arms together again at the front of the table, the edges of the cloth meet, and no one will be aware of the dark secret hidden within.

Seating

Few homes ever have enough seating for every occasion. There will always come a time when you're entertaining a larger number of friends than usual, or when the kids have friends around for tea and you find yourself rummaging around in the shed to salvage dusty deckchairs to supplement the seating arrangements.

So, when you are buying seating for the smaller home, look out for designs which can fold away when not in use, folding chairs and dual-purpose styles of seating are a godsend. Folding chairs need no longer be relegated to the role of seating for the patio or for taking on picnics. Indeed, these days they come in a vast array of styles which are designed for indoor use rather than out. In wood, metal and occasionally plastic, folding chairs are usually light and portable as well as being easy to store when not required. So, if you do not have the space for a permanent dining area, they make ideal dining chairs — or they can simply serve as extra occasional seating when you need it. A table in the sitting room can also double up as a desk or display surface and chairs can be folded away until required.

Finding somewhere for the chairs shouldn't be a problem as they take up very little room when folded flat. They can be stacked in the space under the stairs, in a hall, lobby or wherever you have a bit of redundant space. Or if you would prefer to tidy them away, a floor to ceiling cupboard in the hall will keep them out of sight and can be used to hide away coats, shoes and wellingtons too. If there really is no space for storage, then there is one final solution. Make sure you choose a design which is stylish enough to keep on display all the time, and providing they are not too heavy, you can hang them on the wall!

If you are looking for something really cheap and cheerful, slatted wooden chairs of the type designed for gardens are inexpensive, come in a wide choice of colours and look perfectly stylish enough to use indoors as well as out. They often come as part of a set with a matching table which folds too. As you can purchase a set of four chairs and a table for a very reasonable price, this is a good way of providing temporary dining furniture, especially for the first time home buyer who is short of cash. Once there is the budget for something a little more substantial, this set can be relegated to the garden.

The director's chair, which started out life as a purely utilitarian piece of furniture, has now found its way from behind the camera to perform a starring role in many sitting rooms. Their popularity is hardly surprising as these sturdy seats are cheap to buy, come in a whole array of colours and

look equally at home when pulled up to the dining table as they do in a bedroom , office space or bathroom.

An upholstered stool or ottoman is the ideal piece of extra seating for a sitting room or even a bedroom. You can usually have them covered in the fabric of your choice, so they will fit in with your existing furnishings and a padded top makes them a comfortable spot to rest a weary behind. When not in use as a seat, they can double up as a table for magazines or books, and many models have a hinged top which opens up to provide storage space. Indeed, one clever model on the market is called the 'filo-seat' and it

opens to reveal a filing cabinet as well as storage for more
bulky items. There's even a latticed message board on the
underside of the seat where you can keep postcards, letters
or bills waiting to be paid. Another absolutely ingenious
design is described as a footstool, but is actually designed to
perform two other functions as well. The padded cushion
can be lifted off to leave a solid top which serves as a coffee
table, and then, by removing the top, it opens out, believe it
or not, into a fully sprung 62-cm (25-in) single bed. The
tabletop is used as a headboard and the footstool cushion
acts as a headrest. Perfect for the tiniest room, the footstool
bed is also available in ottoman form, housing a 90-cm or
120-cm (3-ft or 4-ft) bed.

Beds

Sofa-beds have to be one of the cleverest inventions of
recent years. Although they are generally more expensive
than an ordinary sofa, they're really worth the expenditure
when space is at a premium. The thing to remember is that
you get what you pay for. If you only plan to use a sofa-bed
occasionally for overnight guests, then a model from the
cheaper end of the range will suffice. If, however, as a
studio-flat dweller, you will be using a sofa-bed every night,
you will need to buy a quality design which can stand up to
the long-term use. The initial cost of a top-of-the-range
sofa-bed may seem like a large outlay, but when you
consider how much more it will cost to buy both a good
double bed and a sofa, then it falls into perspective, and you
will soon discover it to be money well spent.

There are, of course, much cheaper fold-out beds on the
market. The old faithful Z-bed may rekindle memories of
long, uncomfortable nights spent on creaking springs, but
modern versions of the camp bed are a little more
sophisticated in their design and use of materials. And you
really cannot ignore an idea which is so simple yet really
works — and is cheap into the bargain. A Z-bed is ideal as
an emergency put-you-up when you have an unexpected

The 'Studio Storabed' can serve as a sofa by day and converts to a single or double bed at night. The base pulls out on castors and the legs extend to make twin beds of the same height.

overnight guest, and the rest of the time it can stay folded and hidden under another bed.

If space to store a fold-away bed is scarce, another recent innovation which has found favour, especially for children's rooms, is the conventional single bed which incorporates an extra bed in a drawer under the main mattress. These really are the ultimate bedroom space-savers and could solve the problem in a child's room when a friend comes to stay.

Different cultures have spawned different ways of dealing with the same problems. One such innovation which comes from Japan, and which for once is nothing electronic, is the futon. Based on the same principle as the sofa-bed, the futon differs in that the covered mattress is doubled over on a wooden back and base during the day for seating, and at night the mattress unclips and the base slides forward to give a double bed. Futons also come in single bed sizes and many have added features such as storage drawers underneath and clip-on side tables. It is also claimed that sleeping on a futon, which is much more solid and less flexible than the average mattress, is good for those with bad backs.

Among the many things we have imported from the

French, one not so well known item is the daybed. Daybeds — the name sums them up very neatly — were originally designed for the French aristocracy to catnap on, and were made in wrought iron or wood. They had two ends but only one decorative side — the other side was immaterial as it would always be pushed up against a wall. The most sumptuous designs would have overhead coronas with draperies, tassels and anything else there was room for. At either end, buttoned or tasselled bolster cushions would provide armrests/headrests. It is possible to pick up originals of these designs in this country but they are often very expensive. There are good reproductions and modern interpretations though. If the budget won't run to buying a daybed, you could quickly and easily convert a normal divan by adding a cover, bolsters and cushions to create a bed and sofa in one.

So you see, when space is at a premium, folding furniture provides the quick and easy answer — it won't make your home any bigger, but it can work wonders by allowing you to open up awkward corners and use space which would otherwise be wasted.

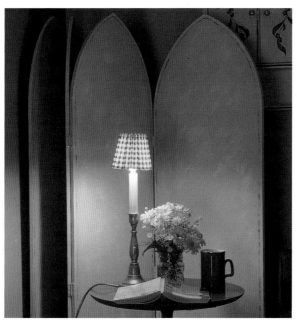

SCREENS

The folding screen is well worth a mention. Much loved by the Victorians for dressing rooms, bedrooms and even sitting rooms, the screen is a simple idea which is much under-used in the modern home.

A screen is a cheap and easy way of dividing one part of a room from the other. If lack of space means you can't have a separate dining room, one way of avoiding having to clear away dinner party remains while guests are still having coffee, is to screen the eating area off from the seating area once the meal is over.

In the bedroom, when there either isn't the space or the budget to fork out for a wardrobe, a screen can be used to hide clothes on hooks or a hanging rail. In kid's rooms too, they can play a valuable role — screening off a homework area or dividing a room occupied by two children so they each have their own space.

Screens can hide a multitude of sins — a boon for the small home owner. And you can paint, paper or upholster them to suit the modern or traditional home.

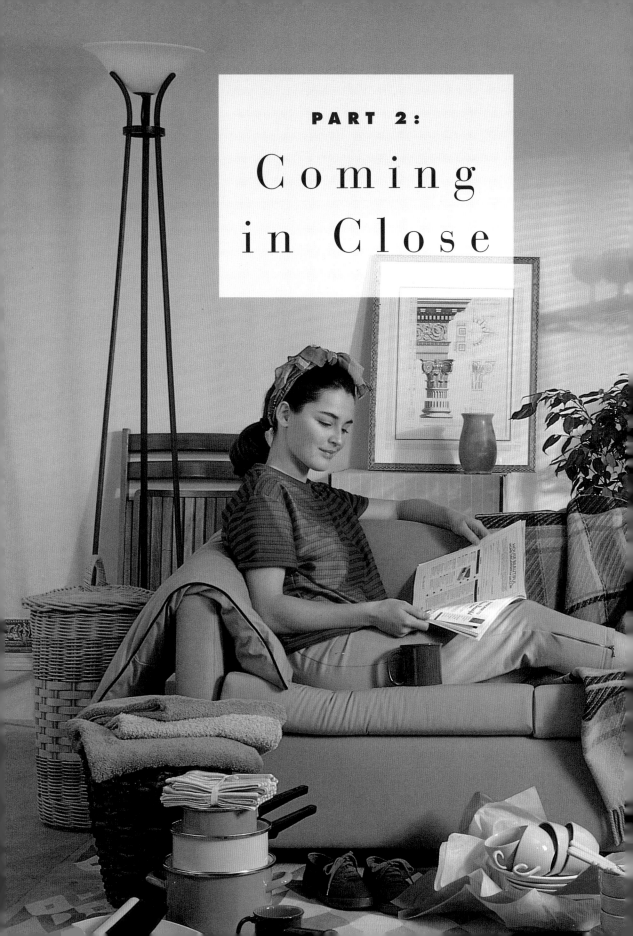

PART 2:
Coming in Close

H A L L

As the first 'room' visitors see when they enter your home, the hall should be warm, inviting and indicative of what's to come throughout the house. Although it can be a difficult and limiting shape to work with, there are ways of decorating and furnishing to overcome this.

It can be hard to feel inspired by what is basically a long corridor with lots of doors opening off it. Often houses built in the 1930s, and more recently, have the advantage over pre-war homes, because they have a square lobby as well as a hall.

But halls are an obvious place to use a little visual trickery and imagination and there are plenty of small pieces of furniture and accessories around which will fit into the limited space. Choose carefully to combine an increased capacity for storage with a stylish touch. The key to creating the right effect is to add details which give points of interest — if there are things to look at, the uninteresting shape becomes irrelevant as the eye is drawn away.

Decorative details

The hall is usually the most complicated and labour intensive area in the home to decorate — so make sure that you get it right, and you won't need to redecorate for a few years. As the hall, stairs and landings are the areas which link all the rooms in the house they should tie in decoratively with your other colour schemes to lead the eye easily from one area to another.

Wallpaper or paint are both viable options for walls. A plain, pale colour is the best choice to lighten up your hall if it's dark and narrow. You can get away with richer, darker colours if it's reasonably wide, but it's best to avoid very busy patterns in such a confined space.

If you do keep walls plain, wallpaper borders are a good way to introduce a little pattern and more colour. Use them at picture rail or dado height and they will help to unify the hall and stairs by leading your eye along the walls. Alternatively, adding a wooden dado rail is a good way of breaking up a large expanse of wall. Use two different papers or paint colours above and below for added interest.

It's worth using an embossed or robust patterned paper below the dado if you want a finish which will withstand wear and tear.

The colour you choose for doors and the skirting is particularly important in the hall. Too much of a contrast will emphasize them, so go for a colour which is near enough to the background colour to blend with it.

Disguise ugly radiators by painting them to match the walls — you could even paint them in stripes if they are against a striped paper. This way they'll fade into the background. Alternatively, install a radiator cover with a decorative fretwork or trellis-like pattern. These covers can be made to size and as well as hiding the radiator they will also give you a small shelf area for a letter rack, telephone or vase of flowers.

FLOORING

Flooring is a major consideration, not just because of the wear and tear it will get, but also because it may be the only feasible way of introducing pattern to this space. Vinyl, linoleum or ceramic tiles are ideal because they are easy to

LEFT: A pleasing arrangement of traditional furnishings provides immediate interest for the visitor to this home. A mirror, barometer and clock, all in dark woods, are centred on the mahogany chest below, which in turn has a radiator concealed behind it.

ABOVE: Shelves of books and ornaments make an eye-catching feature in this hall as they frame the doorway to the sitting room beyond.

**VISUAL
TRICKERY**

*Playing tricks with
your design and
decoration can often
salvage a boring hall.
As we have explained
in Chapter 2 on
Colours and Patterns
there are many simple
ways to make the
wallcoverings and
paint colours you
choose do more than
just look good! Read
on for inspiration.*

● *If your ceiling is
high, add a picture rail
and continue the
ceiling colour down to
meet it. This makes the
ceiling seem lower —
and so the hall
appears warmer and
less lofty.*

● *If your ceiling is low,
wallpaper with vertical
stripes is a possible
solution. The stripes
running from floor to
ceiling trick the eye
into believing that the
ceiling is higher than it
actually is.*

● *If your hall is
particularly long and
you want to make it
seem more compact:
choose a contrasting,
darker colour for the
end walls to bring
them visually closer.*

● *Mirrors are useful in
the hall as they are a
tried and tested way of
making a small area
seem bigger. Use them
on one wall, perhaps
at the far end of the
hall from the door. As
well as reflecting any
available light, in this
position they will also
mirror the complete
hallway.*

clean and hard wearing, but ceramic tiles can make the area feel a little cold. Carpet is less practical, particularly if there are children and pets in the home. If you do choose carpet, have a large doormat which is recessed to make it lie at the same level as the carpet. At least most of the dirt then gets left behind on the mat instead of walked throughout the house. Sisal doormats come in more colours than brown these days, so you may be able to get one which will blend in with your carpet colour.

Another alternative is a floor runner which is long and narrow — specifically designed to suit the shape of a hall. These are back in favour and therefore in production again. You can continue a runner up the stairs and fix it in place with brass stair rods which are also readily available these days in a variety of styles, many based on the original Victorian and Edwardian designs. These can be removed to take the runner up for specialist cleaning when necessary.

LIGHTING

Halls can be difficult to light with all their twists and turns and nooks and crannies. Wall-mounted uplighters or wall washers will project the light upwards giving a consistent level of light and a feeling of continuity throughout the hall and stairs. You could supplement them with a couple of decorative ceiling pendants or even a table lamp or two if you have room for a small table on a landing. Another way of bringing interest and light to a gloomy hall is to hang a gallery of photographs, prints or paintings. You can add picture lights to draw attention to a couple of favourites.

Furniture

The shape of a hall limits you to the type of furniture you can have here, although if it is possible to squeeze in a couple of pieces, this will help to give the area interest. Console tables are ideal for halls, as they have quite narrow tops and often attach to the wall with legs on the front only. You can create an effective focal point by positioning a

Decorative items are crammed into every nook and cranny to make this hallway a room in itself. The piece of wooden fretwork creates an archway and is an unusual way of introducing pattern in a small area.

SPACE SAVERS

● *Don't despair about lack of hanging space for coats — there are brass hooks which originated in ship's cabins, and which fold back against the wall when not in use.*

● *A corner cupboard will fit onto the smallest of landings and give you somewhere to display favourite pieces of china and ornaments.*

● *If your hall really doesn't have room for a table, you could at least have a small decorative shelf. Wall-mounted brackets — either Victorian-style in cast iron or plaster-work corbels — can be topped with a piece of wood, marble or glass.*

console table with a mirror or collection of pictures above it and flanking the whole arrangement with a couple of decorative wall lights. Circular tables with long cloths look stylish on a landing if it is large enough.

In a Victorian or Edwardian hall, a hallstand of the period will really look the part and is practical too — giving you hooks for coats and hats, a slot for umbrellas and often a mirror into the bargain. There are modern hall stands too which take up very little space and give you storage space for just about everything you need to have handy by the front door — boots, shoes, coats, hats, even clips for dog leads. If you have a telephone in the hall, there are tables designed specifically to give you a surface for the phone and somewhere comfortable to sit. Often you will find too, that such a piece of furniture has in-built storage, either as a cupboard underneath or with a seat which lifts up to allow you somewhere to keep phone books.

If you have room for nothing else, a decorative chair with a picture or two above it can be enough to lift this area out of the doldrums.

CASE STUDY

This hall may be tiny, but it provides a warm welcome, and gives an indication of what may be found inside the rest of the house.

PRACTICAL POINTERS

More often than not halls suffer from being dark and dingy and it's quite difficult to think of how best to decorate them to counteract this problem. Fortunately, that is not the case here, for although tiny, this hall has the advantage of several windows as well as a glazed front door. Added to this, all the paintwork is white gloss which makes the interior as light and bright as possible.

The very smart checkerboard floor forms a focal point, attracting your eye and leading the way through into the sitting room. Vinyl tiles like these are easy to find, fairly inexpensive and eminently practical for a hallway, where wet and muddy feet can be the order of the day. A painted wooden garden chair looks perfectly at home here and provides a place to sit while you remove tight fitting wellies, or if you just want to watch the world go by.

Behind the front door, there is just room for an old bentwood hatstand where dripping coats and umbrellas can be left before entering the rest of the house. If you don't have room for a hatstand, a row of brass hooks will serve just the same purpose.

DECORATIVE DETAILS

It is important to think of the hall as another room, rather than just a corridor leading to the rest of the house. And even when there isn't room to fit in furniture, a few well chosen accessories can make all the difference and give it character. Here, two stone urns of flowers provide the perfect welcome and give pleasing symmetry to the entrance. You could equally well use two bay trees or conifers in tubs.

Once inside there are several unusual objects to catch the eye and interest the visitor. The front door is propped open with a stone bust, and an old stoneware jar contains a varied selection of antique walking sticks. The battered leather suitcase looks as if someone may be about to take it on holiday, but in fact, it holds the various odds and ends used for gardening.

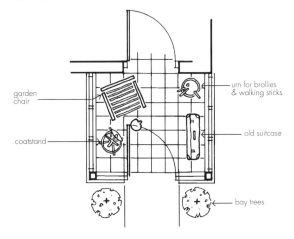

garden chair

coatstand

urn for brollies & walking sticks

old suitcase

bay trees

AT A GLANCE

• This charming hall has a countrified air even though it is in a town.

• A pair of stone urns planted up with pelargoniums and lobelia give a splash of colour to the front of the house.

• A delightful checkered floor entices you inside. The vinyl tiles are eminently practical too.

• A painted wooden garden chair fits in perfectly and can be moved out into the garden on sunnier days.

• A hefty doorstop is essential for propping open a glazed door. Here, a stone bust performs the task admirably.

• There is just room for a bentwood hatstand behind the front door where dripping coats and hats can be left.

• A collection of antique walking sticks and a battered leather suitcase add interest without taking up too much space.

LIVING / DINING ROOM

'Living room' is a broad definition. How you actually use your living space depends on your lifestyle. But one thing's for sure, as the area where most leisure time is spent at home, it has to be adaptable and durable.

The living room often has to serve several different purposes. Relaxing, whether to read, listen to music or watch TV are the most usual, but it may also be the room where the family eats, where the kids do their homework and where you sit down to pay the bills, write letters or indulge in a hobby such as sewing. It will certainly be a room where the family congregate, so furnishings need to be pretty hardwearing. Of course, it is also usually the room that visitors see — your public face — so you will most certainly want it to be comfortable and inviting, and to display a certain degree of style.

Decorative details

As we explained in Chapter 2, the colours, textures and patterns we introduce into a room have a profound influence, and nowhere is this more important than in the living room. If you use your living room a lot during the day, then you will probably want to open it up, making it feel as

This space is used for living, dining and cooking for a family, so it has to be adaptable. The antique country pine furniture won't suffer from a few more knocks and scratches and the vinyl flooring is hard-wearing too. The choice of light, fresh colours and details such as the lattice-work on the wall units makes the room decorative as well as functional.

light and spacious as possible. If, however, you are out at work and the living room gets most use in the evenings for watching TV or reading, then you may prefer to create a cosy looking room with darker, richer colours which looks its best in electric light.

The colours for a daytime room should be light and easy on the eye. If the room gets a lot of sun or natural light, greens and blues will look fresh and light. But if the room has a northerly aspect, choose from the warmer end of the spectrum — soft yellow, cream, peach or pink.

Pattern must be carefully selected if your room is small. Highly patterned walls are probably out — large patterns look their best on a wide expanse of wall where you can see the pattern repeat properly and smaller, very detailed patterns can often look too frantic. It is much better to use regular pattern such as vertical stripes which are not only pleasing to the eye, but also make the room seem taller.

Life in this studio flat is all based in one open space so there is a continuity of design and colour throughout. The large pine table is used for everything from serving dinner for six to sewing and doing the accounts.

TYPES OF LIGHT FITTING

● *Pendant lights: the most common light fittings in homes, they usually hang by a flex from the centre of the ceiling. Useful for general lighting.*

● *Wall-lights: wall-mounted fittings which direct and diffuse light in a variety of ways depending on the material of the housing. Useful for general, accent and information lighting.*

● *Wall-washers: recessed ceiling lights which bathe walls in a stream of accent lighting.*

● *Uplighters: these project light upwards and bounce illumination off the ceiling. Used for general and accent lighting. Often freestanding and portable, otherwise they come in the form of wall-lights.*

● *Spotlights: these adaptable fittings can be mounted on the ceiling, walls and even the floor, using lengths of lighting track. Great for accent lighting.*

● *Standard and table lamps: freestanding, portable fittings of variable height that can sit on a floor or surface to enhance any general or accent lighting scheme.*

● *Desk lamps: provide task light where you want it.*

Wallpaper featuring a simple motif in a vertical repeat, for example a fleur de lys, a leaf pattern or something similar, will also work well.

On a practical note, if you have children and pets around, do choose hard wearing furnishings in colours which don't show the dirt too easily and are easy to clean when they do get grubby.

LIGHTING

Lighting can make or break your design scheme. It highlights or disguises the room's features, defines its colours and contours and generally helps to create the background mood, so you have to know how to make it work for you.

You can mix a variety of light sources in a living room to create a warm mood or a dramatic effect, depending on what you are using it for at any given time. One way to make the most of a ceiling pendant light is where you have a dining area which you use for formal entertaining as well as family meals. Fitting a rise and fall mechanism to a ceiling pendant above the dining table allows you to bring it down to create an intimate pool of light when entertaining friends, but still have the option of using it as a general purpose light at other times.

Wall uplighters are another source of good general light, and will lend a little more drama to a room than a central pendant. Light washes the walls and bounces off the ceiling, creating effective areas of shadow. You can buy these in many different designs and most adaptable are the semi-circular plaster models which can be painted — either a plain colour to match the walls behind them, or with a pattern to make them more of a feature.

Table and standard lamps create warm pools of light and can be placed at various points around the room. They are favoured by most people because they also look decorative and the shades can be matched to other soft furnishings in the room.

There are various ways to highlight specific items or areas depending on the effect you want to create and what the light is needed for. Small spotlights or recessed ceiling lights can draw attention to a collection of china, a group of plants or a favourite picture. Clip-on picture lights are another easy way to light a favourite painting or print. For desks and work areas you will need task lighting to make sure you have a powerful source of light so that you can direct it straight onto the job in hand.

FURNITURE

As few homes these days have the space for a separate dining room, the living room will often include a dining table and chairs which are perhaps only used for formal entertaining or large family get-togethers, with everyday meals being eaten in the kitchen. A dining table can have fold-down flaps or an extra leaf to adapt to small and larger numbers. If you never entertain on a large scale, buy a small table which can sit against the wall.

Adaptability is the key to success when you're short on space. In this living/dining room, linen placemats, silver cutlery and glowing candles turn an everyday table into something special.

A quirky recess in an old cottage is put to very good use as an unusual dining area.

If your taste is more contemporary, a dining table on trestles might be a good solution. This type of table has the advantage of being fairly hardwearing, of being easily dismantled if not in regular use and is also relatively inexpensive. It's certainly a good interim measure if you're short on cash, and can be relegated to a workroom if and when you move and acquire more space.

It is also possible to buy tables, both rectangular and round which can be heightened for dining and lowered again for use as a coffee table. And folding chairs are available in many, much more stylish designs than in the past, and take up very little space when not in use.

SEATING

As it is a room which is primarily used for leisure, a major requirement of the living room is comfortable seating — a sofa or two and perhaps a couple of easy chairs. It makes sense to make this furniture work for you. Anything you can buy which serves more than one purpose eases space problems.

It is currently more fashionable to have two sofas rather than the traditional three-piece suite, but one or two armchairs and a small sofa may be easier to fit in depending on how you want to arrange your furniture. Smaller pieces of furniture are also much more flexible and don't limit you to one layout.

A wooden trunk or blanket chest is a really useful piece of furniture for virtually any room in the house. It gives you a flat surface which can become a table or a seat, and has the added advantage of storage space underneath. A fabric-covered foam cushion will provide a little more comfort and if you don't need the extra seating all the time, this can be stored inside to give you a table top for such things as drinks and magazines.

Victorian houses often have bay windows. This space is rarely put to very good use and is an ideal place to site a piece of purpose-built furniture. The three-sided shape will accommodate a fair sized shelving unit or, even better, a window seat. Foam cushions covered in an upholstery fabric will be hard wearing and can be removed for cleaning and, underneath the seat, a number of cupboards will give you useful storage space.

Leisure pursuits will dictate the other pieces of furniture to be found in your living room. There may be a piano in a musical home. If board games or cards are your thing then

HIRING HELP

● *The best way to find out about any kind of builder, decorator or craftsman is by recommendation from someone you know. Otherwise, consult your local paper or Yellow Pages under 'Joinery Manufacturers'.*

● *If they are members of The Guild of Master Craftsmen this is a fairly good indication of the standard of their work.*

● *Always pay a visit to their showroom, if they have one, ask to see a portfolio of work and ideally have a look at a similar job carried out in another home.*

● *A joiner will visit to talk to you about what you want and to measure up. He will then give you a quote and should supply drawings before starting work to give you an idea of how the finished job will look.*

● *If you feel unsure about any aspect of the design now is the time to speak. He will be unhappy and you will be out of pocket if you start changing your mind halfway through the job.*

you may want space for a small games table. If you work from home or the children do their homework here then an alcove may be occupied by a small desk. These are all elements to be taken into account when planning the layout of your furniture.

Storage

Most homes these days have to find a place for technology in some shape or form. A television and video, a radio or music centre and perhaps a computer are all trappings of modern-day living which need to be slotted into our living rooms without dominating them completely. This creates a dilemma for those who prefer traditional surroundings — these uniformly black and chrome machines don't sit happily in anything other than a hi-tech interior. So disguising or hiding them is usually preferable.

Smaller televisions can be supported on a swing bracket which allows you to fold them back into a cupboard or corner when not in use. And manufacturers of reproduction furniture have risen admirably to the challenge of designing cabinets to hold TV, video and your selection of cassettes as well. So what looks like a Queen-Anne cupboard is, in fact, a marrying of the ancient and modern as it modestly conceals innumerable wires, dials and your complete collection of Fawlty Towers tapes. Old pine cupboards too, can often be custmomized to suit this purpose.

Side tables and coffee tables should have shelving or a cupboard underneath so that they can provide storage space as well as a useful surface. A coffee table which has a glazed recess in the top gives you somewhere to display favourite knick-knacks or breakables. So as well as having a coffee table, you also have a conversation piece.

Most people need some shelf space to hold books, to display favourite objects and ornaments, or simply to keep clutter off the floor. Cupboards, of course, are neater, allowing you to hide paraphernalia away and presenting a uniform and united front, rather than the diversity of a mix of items on shelves. But a row of cupboards can look very blank and characterless, so it is best to opt for a mix of the two. You can then use your shelves for display and banish the piles of paperwork or stacks of cassettes out of sight behind closed doors.

A wide range of shelving is available and what you select will depend largely on your taste, your budget and also on what type of storage you really need. Flat-pack units are the most inexpensive way to buy shelving and the fact that they are free-standing means you can take them with you when you move.

At the other end of the scale are custom-built units. The advantage with these is that they can be designed to suit your specific requirements and built to fit into alcoves or along a stretch of wall which gives a much more permanent appearance. If, however, they are fixed you will have to leave them if you move, and of course, because they are custom-designed they will be much more pricey than something off the peg. There are many companies who specialize in this type of work — they often build kitchens and bedroom furniture too.

CASE STUDY

This living room is a good example of what you can do with a very limited space — it is part of a tiny house which measures only 9ft wide!

PRACTICAL POINTERS

The owner of this living room has been totally undaunted by the lack of space and in an area measuring about 2.7m (9 ft) square has managed to fit in a table and chairs, a fireplace, two shelving units and — on the opposite wall — a dresser filled with china as well.

The circular pine table, with its matching chairs, forms the main focal point and is a good choice in this small area as it will seat more people than an equivalent square table and can be pushed towards a corner of the room. The french

windows let in plenty of light and, when open during the summer, lead out to a small, but pretty garden which gives the living area an increased feeling of space.

The walls and ceiling, which are painted a warm buttermilk colour, provide a light, clean contrast to the varied elements which line the walls of the room. In fact, as the rooms in this house are all so small, the

creamy wall colour is used throughout for continuity and to promote a feeling of spaciousness. The oatmeal carpet is also a fairly good base colour to use throughout the house as it will suit most rooms. At night, lighting comes from two sources — a rise and fall lamp over the dining table and a smaller lamp sitting on the mantelpiece.

DECORATIVE DETAILS

Even though there isn't a chimney breast in the room, a pretty Art Nouveau fireplace looks perfectly at home against one wall and has its non-operational grate filled with pine cones instead of coal or logs. A carefully positioned pine shelf unit above it adds visual weight so that the missing chimney breast almost goes unnoticed. The shelves and mantelpiece are crammed with postcards, knick knacks and other personal effects proving that you can have clutter in a small space so long as it is 'organized' clutter and limited to one or two areas.

Pine furniture, frilled curtains and carefully chosen accessories all give this room a very cottagey feel which suits its small proportions.

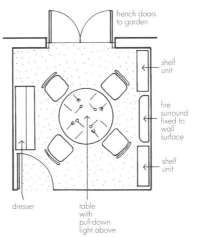

french doors to garden

shelf unit

fire surround fixed to wall surface

shelf unit

dresser

table with pull-down light above

KITCHEN

Small but perfectly formed — a neat, petite kitchen can hide a multitude of things. Cupboards that turn inside out, tables that collapse, magic storage carousels — the disappearing tricks are endless. All you need is a little inspiration and a lot of careful planning.

Kitchens were the success story of the 1980s in the good planning stakes. Designers and manufacturers set themselves the task of squeezing just about any space-saving idea or gadget you care to think of into this, the most well-used of rooms in the home. The fitted kitchen can now be all things to all people — somewhere to cook, eat, wash, iron and much, much more. Of particular benefit to the owner of the small home, these days lack of space really need not be a problem.

Your budget no longer has to be limitless either. Although it is all too easy to spend thousands of pounds on a fitted kitchen, you can equally spend a small amount and end up with a kitchen which is stylish, well organized and a pleasure to work and live in.

So where do you start? Well, this will depend on the look you are after but what you choose in the end will be dictated to, largely, by what you can afford to spend. On every high street and the outskirts of every town there are specialist kitchen companies, retail kitchen chains and large DIY stores, all with variations on the theme. Your starting point should be to pay a few of them a visit to find out what style of units and what kind of service is on offer. If you don't like the units you've got and are working to a really limited budget, the Sunday papers are full of companies who will simply supply you with replacement doors.

Unless you choose to follow the DIY route, you will usually be provided with the services of a kitchen planner. By and large this is an advantage. They have done it all before, know how to solve given problems and know what can be done with their product. Unfortunately, the kitchen planner can sometimes be more of a hazard than a help — we know of situations where the homeowner has ended up advising the planner, when he or she seems to be having trouble getting it right. Thankfully, however, this is rare.

REMEMBER TO INCLUDE ON YOUR PLAN

- *Any architectural features such as chimney breasts.*

- *Doors and the direction in which they open.*

- *Window dimensions — width, height, height of sill where relevant.*

- *Ceiling height.*

- *Where you want tiling — allow for extra height above hobs.*

- *Gas pipes.*

- *Power points.*

The owner of this tiny kitchen has to make good use of base units — there isn't room for wall cupboards. Clever touches such as the circular sink and flap down cooker top ensure there is as much worktop space as possible.

Nevertheless, it does no harm to equip yourself with some of the basics of kitchen planning which will allow you to ask the right questions and to make sure you get what you want when the planner comes around. Of course, if you are doing-it-yourself, a lesson in planning is all the more vital.

Decorative details

The style of units you choose will depend on your taste and there are all kinds of designs and finishes from country pines to slick city lacquers from which to make your choice. If your kitchen is small then something with a light finish will be preferable.

White is traditionally credited with creating an illusion of space, and makes a natural choice for smaller kitchens. There's no need to sacrifice practicality to style though — a protective varnish or lacquer finish will make it easier to keep white cabinets clean. It's best if appliances match the white of the units, while sinks — traditionally stainless steel or neutral in colour — look more integrated when set into a worktop of a similar shade.

MEASURING UP

● *Take several measurements as the ceiling height and walls might not be constant — use a retractable steel tape measure.*

● *It's important to measure the height of the ceiling as many manufacturers make wall cupboards in two different heights.*

● *A handy tip is to rest the end of the tape measure on the floor. Feed the bulk of the tape to the ceiling and double it over when it reaches the top. Lock the tape, lower it and read the height off at the point where it doubles over.*

● *You may be offered a choice of cupboard sizes but standard unit sizes you can expect to find are 500mm, 600mm and 1,000mm.*

● *Most appliances are a standard size of 600mm except fridges which vary from slimline versions to vast larder fridges.*

Here's a great solution for the kitchen which is short on floor and wall space. A clever overhead rack has been built to store pots and pans and as it continues downwards, it also incorporates a plate rack and shelves.

MEASURING UP

continued . . .

- *Allow room to manoeuver appliances for maintenance without forcing — exactly 600mm may not be enough.*

- *If you want to draw up your own plan, use squared paper with each square representing, say, 30cms (1ft) and cut out shapes to represent your units and appliances.*

Introducing a little colour will avoid a clinical effect, and if you stick to a limited palette it won't overpower a confined area. Using just one or two shades for tiles, flooring, walls and accessories, you should find it easy to create a stylish balance that offsets the furniture. But, of course, it takes more than clever use of colour to create space — real or illusionary.

ORGANIZATION

If you are investing in new units or just trying to reorganize your existing ones, there are plenty of inventive and inexpensive ideas which will help you out. Plate stackers, for example, are multi-tiered racks which allow you to stack plates, bowls and saucers above, but not on top of, one another — so making it easy to extract a couple of plates from the bottom without disrupting the whole pile. Drawer dividers are sturdy, plastic sections which can be arranged to suit your requirements and will hold all those oddly shaped kitchen utensils which always seem to get tangled up with one another in a drawer. Expanding shelves are placed at the back of cupboards to elevate small bottles and jars so you can see what you've got instead of having to rummage around only to find a sauce bottle which is well past its sell-by date!

Small kitchens don't have to mean cramped kitchens. Whether you are about to have a total re-design or simply upgrade what you've got, there is no excuse for not having a well-designed hub of the home.

Above all, try to enjoy the benefits of your small space kitchen. If it is carefully designed, it may be more practical to run than a large kitchen as everything is close at hand. And remember, economy sized appliances often mean economy sized bills!

SPACE SAVERS

● *Small spaces can be used effectively as tray recesses/towel rails. Anything smaller than 200mm however, is impractical.*

● *Fit baskets, shelves and carousels inside cupboards to maximise every inch of space. These will usually come as part of a fitted kitchen, but you can buy them separately from some sources.*

● *Hanging rails and racks are a great way of keeping worksurfaces clear and provide extra display areas too.*

LEFT: In the smaller kitchen, appliances should be disguised behind unit doors to keep the area neat.

ABOVE: Even waste-disposal can be done with a flourish in the kitchen of the 1990s. Waste is swept into the bin sited beneath a recessed lid in the worktop.

CASE STUDY

In spite of its size, all the elements essential to a working kitchen have been incorporated in the design of this tiny area. In fact, this mini kitchen has distinct advantages — not only is everything close at hand, but it takes only the minimum of effort to keep things clean.

PRACTICAL POINTERS

To make the most of every inch of available space, this kitchen is built in a U-shape that provides units and worktops on three sides and also divides the area effectively from the sitting room. There's room for a freestanding microwave, and a wooden chopping board fits neatly over the sink drainer to provide a useful extra work surface.

Efficient clothes-washing and drying facilities are vital in any home — especially if you have young children — and a combined washer-drier is a practical way of saving space in a small kitchen like this. Here the machine is concealed behind a hinged panel so that it is completely hidden from sight, and blends in with the units.

The fridge is dealt with in the same way, by choosing a compact model which fits neatly into the run of units. By disguising it behind a drawer and door fascia, it blends in discreetly with the cupboards.

An extractor fan is vital to prevent cooking smells from reaching the living area of the studio. So a cooker hood has been integrated with the line of wall cupboards, and also has storage space above it for pots and pans.

DECORATIVE DETAILS

Here is proof — if you needed it — that there's no need for a small kitchen to look utilitarian and cramped. Clever planning has provided this area — measuring less than 3m (10ft) square — with everything necessary for a kitchen as well as a diner.

From the sitting room, the striking combination of limed wood and sparkling wall tiles presents an attractive view. The pale wood maintains a light and airy look for the kitchen and blends well with the fresh white and blues used in the living area.

Design details of this kitchen such as the glass-fronted wall cupboards, open plate-racks and end shelves break up the solid run of wooden fronts and provide space for displaying ornaments.

Light plays an important role in such a small room. Spot-bulbs and under-cupboard pelmet strips are used to supplement the natural daylight from the overhead skylight.

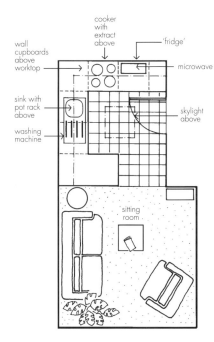

wall cupboards above worktop

cooker with extract above

'fridge'

microwave

sink with pot rack above

skylight above

washing machine

sitting room

AT A GLANCE

• This well-planned kitchen contains everything you need for living/dining in an area measuring just 3m (10ft) square.

• As the kitchen is in one 'arm' of an L-shaped room, the host or hostess can enjoy the company of guests while cooking.

• Functional appliances are concealed behind integrated door panels. This is particularly important if the kitchen is 'on view' from another room.

• Fitted to ceiling height, wall cupboards make full use of the available space in a low-ceilinged room.

• Tongue-and-groove cladding delineates the kitchen from the living area.

• A brass rail set at worktop level for hanging cloths over takes up very little space.

• The tiled worktops and splashbacks are decorative and practical.

BEDROOM

Bedrooms often get a raw deal when it comes to planning and decorating. So long as there is somewhere to sleep and hang a few clothes, we don't tend to think much further about how we can best use the space. But if your bedroom feels no bigger than a boxroom, perhaps it's time to follow our advice for making more of your room at the top.

The bedroom is where we spend up to a third of our lives, and not just for sleeping. We want to relax, read, maybe watch TV, and reflect on the day just ending and the one to come. This room should be somewhere we can be ourselves and as such should be an inviting and comfortable place. But because the neighbours aren't likely to see it, the bedroom often gets relegated to the bottom of the organizational stakes. So if you're sick of clothes crammed into insubstantial wardrobes, dusty suitcases under the bed and piles of books balanced on the bedside table then follow our guide to using your space more inventively.

The fitted bedroom

Bedrooms are receiving much more attention from the professional planners these days — as a follow-up to the fitted kitchen, we now have the fitted bedroom. For many people this is the ideal — call in the experts, explain your requirements and the next thing you know, the whole problem of storage and space saving is solved for you, with a place for everything and everything in its place.

The designs from these companies, although varied in style and finish, should provide you with a comprehensive and well-planned mixture of storage space — hanging rails, shelves, shoe racks, small rails for ties and scarves, overhead cupboards for hats, bags and smaller items of luggage and there will usually be a full-length mirror incorporated too.

Another option for a fitted bedroom is to have the whole thing custom-designed and built by a joiner. The advantage here is that everything is based specifically on your bedroom and your requirements. As the whole system will be built from scratch, there is more flexibility and you will end up with a design which is special to you. It will, however, cost you quite a bit more than a modular system.

In each of these cases, there will be a professional on

This bedroom system is called 'Convert a room' and that just about says it all. Only one of the wardrobes is actually what it seems. Pull the handles of the small overhead cupboards and hey presto, a bed folds down.

USING A FITTED BEDROOM SPECIALIST

● *You are almost spoilt for choice about who to go to these days although your final choice will probably be decided by what you can afford to spend. At one end of the scale are the very upmarket specialist kitchen companies who have diversified into bedrooms. Some will not only supply the cabinetry for your bedroom but will devise a colour scheme, have curtains made up and supply carpet too, if you can afford it.*

● *At the other end are the large furniture store chains on out-of-town sites, who offer fitted bedrooms and kitchens as just one aspect of their business. In between, there are many other companies and types of services. It pays to shop around, look at what's on offer and get an idea of cost before you commit yourself.*

● *Based on a modular system, like that of a kitchen, you can select what you like to suit your requirements. Some ranges are sometimes totally built-in — and others look fitted, but are in fact movable.*

● *The company will usually send a planner along to look at your space and talk to you about what you need.*

hand to guide you and make the best use of your space, but it will help if you have had a look around a showroom or seen a catalogue in advance so that you can get an idea of what's available. A run of fitted units can often incorporate your bed, so that the whole look becomes streamlined. Decorative details can be added such as shelving which is run down each side of the bed ending at bedside tables; and cupboards can often be run across above the bed to give you extra storage where otherwise the space might be wasted.

The unfitted bedroom

But what do you do if you either can't afford, or indeed don't like, the fitted look? Well, the key here is to organize your space to make the most of what you've got and perhaps add an item or two of free-standing furniture. Ranges of fitted furniture often include matching free-standing items such as dressing tables, bedside tables, bedheads and the like. You may choose to buy one or two of these individual pieces rather than go for the entire fitted look. You will often find that even these small pieces might incorporate integral items such as a concealed laundry basket.

The big advantage, of course, with free-standing furniture is that you can take it with you if you move — and if you have spent time and money getting what you want, you will probably choose to take it to your next home.

Furniture

Beds come in all sizes and your comfort is the most important aspect when choosing one. A good bed should last a lifetime, as should a good quality mattress, providing you treat them well. Before you buy a bed, make sure you try out several within your price range so that you end up buying the best you can for your money.

Obviously, the style of bed you choose is a purely personal thing, but if you decide to go for a divan, then try and select one with drawers in the base. These, particularly

The unusual shape of this small bedroom is turned into a feature by emphasizing its twists and turns with a wallpaper border.

those on a double bed, will give you a good amount of concealed storage space which can take over from the piles of suitcases on top of the wardrobe and the boxes under the bed — or at least supplement them!

If you aren't in the market for a new bed, you'll have to adapt what you've got, and that means reorganizing the jumble underneath the bed. Aside from being a bit of a dust-trap, this space is actually quite useful — most of us make use of it, but a bit haphazardly. So instead of shoving old boxes, bags and suitcases under it, invest in some proper storage solutions which really will make the most of the space you've got and will keep their contents dust-free. There are various types of plastic or vinyl stacking boxes now on the market, which are produced in several alternative sizes suitable for storing different types of clothes, linens and other types of bedding. They are particularly useful for out-of-season clothes or spare bedding which you only need access to occasionally.

continued . . .

● *A plan, often computerized, will then be drawn up for your approval.*

● *Providing you agree the design and the price, the company will then deliver your goods and install them for you.*

SPACE SAVERS

● *Use three- or four-drawer chests as bedside tables.*

● *A blanket box or chest of some kind provides a useful surface for the morning tea tray, and it can be used to hold clothes and bedding too. A fabric-covered foam cushion made to fit the top will brighten it up.*

WARDROBES

If your wardrobe is a complete disaster area — doors won't shut because you've got too much crammed in and when you do get anything out it needs ironing before you can wear it — you may like to know that there are gadgets galore to help you make better use of that space.

Hanger spacers are lengths of ribbed plastic which slip over your wardrobe hanging rail to prevent hangers from

No room for a wardrobe? No problem. Just build a platform for your bed and hang your clothes underneath!

sliding together, thus putting an end to crushed clothes. Extending hanger holders will support several items of clothing at once and hang them in a graduated line so that you are making more of the wasted space at the bottom of the wardrobe. Another way to use this spare space under short items like jackets and blouses, is to add another hanging bar — you can buy rails which simply hook onto your main hanging rail or you can make one with a length of chrome tubing and two supports, both of which you can buy at DIY stores. If you want to leave half of the space for longer dresses and coats, divide the base of the wardrobe into two, with a 90–120-cm (3–4-ft) high piece of chipboard and attach the half rail between this and one side of the wardrobe. Hat boxes are back in vogue so rather than piling suitcases on top of the wardrobe, stack a set of pretty hat boxes there instead. Available in a variety of colours and patterns — mostly floral — they come in a selection of sizes to hold anything you wish from belts to undies — and hats, of course.

Another idea for the well-organized wardrobe are shoe racks which come in a number of sizes and designs, to stand in the bottom of the wardrobe and even to hang on the back of a door. Or as an alternative, how about using a plastic, stacking vegetable rack in the bottom of your wardrobe for shoes, hats, scarves or anything else small enough to get jumbled up?

Hanging rails with hooks which clip on to the backs of bedroom doors are another nifty idea which will give you enough space for three or four outfits, and will help ease the squeeze when friends come to stay.

If you don't have room for a full-sized wardrobe, then a hanging chest might be enough for you. These come in a selection of styles — mostly traditional in pine or mahogany finishes. They look like a chest of drawers but open out to reveal hanging space along with drawer space too. The drawback is that they will not store anything longer than jackets and shirts.

continued . . .

● *Few of us need a spare bedroom very often — the occasional overnight guest doesn't really merit turning your only spare space over for this purpose. So why not make your spare bedroom double up as a workroom too? There are ranges of fitted furniture on the market which allow you to do just that. A run of units incorporating open shelves and cupboard space during the day, can be transformed at the flick of a switch to a fold-out bed surrounded by shelving. What seemed like floor-length cupboards are actually the length of the bed and two top 'cupboards' become the bed end. Your guests will not only be offered hospitality and comfort, but they might also get the sneaking feeling they are playing a part in a James Bond movie!*

CASE STUDY

This snug little bedroom has to work extra hard space-wise, for not only is it somewhere cosy to sleep, but by day it becomes a sitting room too.

PRACTICAL POINTERS

The comfy double bed is quickly transformed into a sofa, when the duvet and pillows are removed and the mattress folded away. The bedlinens are stored in the chest on the left — which during the day becomes a television table. But in a room this size, where do you find space to put a wardrobe? The simple answer is that you don't — you'll have to come up with a more inventive alternative. So, how about a freestanding clothes-rail — like those used in shops? As well as clothes on hangers, two lightweight nylon hanging racks, one for shoes and small items, the other for bulkier clothes like sweaters. They are attached to the clothes-rail with Velcro strips. Hide the whole rack away behind a folding screen during the day. A small circular table and upholstered foot-stool give more useful surface for both bedroom and living room.

DECORATIVE DETAILS

A homemade pegboard-cum-shelf runs the width of the room to provide invaluable storage and display space. The pegs can hang a myriad of things from clothes and towels to a pretty, painted cupboard. This opens to reveal doors which are mirrored on the inside — a clever hideaway dressing table, are the perfect place to store toiletries and other bits and pieces.

The cream-coloured floor-covering keeps the mood of the room light and bright. It is made from an unusual mix of sisal and wool which makes it extremely hard-wearing and very soft underfoot — an ideal combination for a room which has to double as living room and bedroom. For bedtime reading, the pretty candle lamps with gingham shades cast a warm glow, and their narrow bases mean they take up little of the limited surface space when not in use during the day.

• A smart double sofa-bed offers comfortable sitting by day and sleeping by night.

• Bedlinen is stored in a wooden chest which doubles up as a TV table.

• Instead of a wardrobe, a freestanding clothes-rail provides hanging space for clothes.

• Sturdy nylon hanging shelves give space to fold jumpers, store shoes, etc.

• A folding screen looks decorative and you can hide the clothes-rail behind it too.

• A painted wooden shelf-cum-pegboard has shelf space above for storage and display and knobs below for hanging anything from clothes to cupboards.

• An upholstered footstool can double up as a seat or an occasional table.

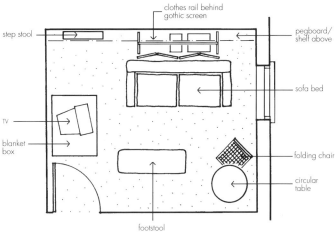

step stool

clothes rail behind gothic screen

pegboard/ shelf above

sofa bed

TV

blanket box

folding chair

circular table

footstool

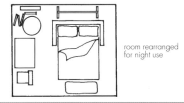

room rearranged for night use

BATHROOM

The bathroom should be a place for private retreat. Somewhere you can feel comfortable and indulge yourself — not easy if there isn't enough room to swing a wet flannel!

Because the time we spend in them is minimal, bathrooms are often low on the list of priorities when it comes to allocating space in the home. They also suffer from being very static rooms — we can't swop the furniture round when we tire of the layout. So it's important to get the planning right from the start to make the most of the space we've got.

If you are planning a bathroom from scratch you have a distinct advantage. You can select sanitaryware in a colour and shape you like and site it where it will make the most of the available space. If, however, you are trying to make your mark on an inherited bathroom without ripping out the existing fittings, then you have to be more cunning.

PLANNING THE SPACE

If you are planning a complete re-fit, it may be worth asking around or advertising in the local paper to see if you can find any takers for the suite you are about to remove. Even if you don't get much money for it, at least it will not go to waste and may be the answer to someone else's prayers.

Finding new sanitaryware should be your first task. You can, if your budget allows, call in a bathroom expert at this point. You will find bathroom and kitchen showrooms in many high streets and the advantage here is that they will often advise and guide you as to what is available in tiles, wallcoverings and floorings as well as sanitaryware. They will come and measure up, look at your budget and fit the whole thing for you — all you have to do is make your choices and pay the bill.

If you prefer to research the market yourself, look around at the choice of bathroom suites available. It's an advantage to visit a large showroom where you can see many different designs on display on the one site. The DIY 'sheds', found on the outskirts of most big towns, are worth a visit as the prices will be about the lowest you will find

and designs are becoming ever more varied. Get hold of
brochures where possible as these usually give dimensions
which will help when planning your layout. The colour you
select comes down to personal preference but although
fashions for coloured sanitaryware come and go, we would
always advise you to choose white. It won't limit you when
you decide to redecorate and never dates.

Drawing up a plan is vital for a small bathroom and you

A highly patterned
wallpaper works
surprisingly well in this small
bathroom. Its success is
based on the fact that
everything else in the room
is kept relatively plain and
simple.

DRAWING A PLAN

● *Bear in mind that moving plumbing isn't always easy or possible. Water supplies can usually be shifted around without too much trouble, but the loo can't, as it must be connected directly to the main soil stack that runs down the back or side of the house.*

● *Measure the space and decide on a simple scale, eg one square of graph paper = 30cms (1ft).*

● *Draw the room onto your graph paper, marking existing plumbing, doors, windows, lights, alcoves, etc.*

● *Working to the same scale, draw and cut out simple squares or rectangles to represent each of the elements you hope to include, eg bath, loo, washbasin, shower, bidet.*

● *Try these shapes in various positions on your plan to find the best positions for the various appliances.*

● *Allow enough space to move around each piece. You'll need about 90cms (3ft) in front of the basin, at the side of the bath and in front of the loo or shower cubicle.*

may be surprised just how much you fit in when you swop things around. You can do-it-yourself using squared paper and cut out paper shapes to represent the bathroom suite, or there are several bathroom companies who can supply bathroom planning grids to use with their own ranges of sanitaryware. Although most loos and basins come in fairly standard sizes, there are smaller than normal baths and corner baths which may help if you are really short on space. You should have an idea of the models you are going to choose before starting on your plan.

Decorative details

If you are stuck with badly organized existing fixtures and fittings because of a limited budget, there are still ways of making your bathroom appear bigger. The most obvious way is with colour — painting the walls will have a dramatic and immediate effect. But remember to choose one of the steam-proof ranges specially designed for bathrooms and kitchens. If you decide to use a wallpaper, it's best to select from a range designed for bathrooms and stick all wallcoverings with a paste containing fungicide.

White walls will make a small bathroom seem more spacious but can feel chilly — it's preferable to choose a soft cream or pale yellow which are warmer, or perhaps a pale blue or green which have a natural association with water and are also restful colours. Alternatively, you could choose to ignore the space limitations altogether and make a virtue of your bathroom's enclosed character by using a rich, dark, warm colour — rust, ochre or olive, for example — to exaggerate the effect of a cosy, private haven. If you're keeping walls plain, add a stencilled border along the side of the bath panel or at picture rail height to introduce some pattern, or try out a paint technique on the walls such as sponging or rag-rolling — this will add textural interest and camouflage bumpy or uneven surfaces.

If you're stuck with a sanitaryware colour you hate, change the emphasis by introducing another,

complementary colour in the form of a
roller blind, shower curtain, towels and
other accessories. Remove the side panel
from the bath and replace it with tongue
and groove panelling or a sheet of
medium density fibreboard to which you
can fix lengths of wooden moulding for a
traditional panelled look. You can then
paint the surface a colour you prefer, to
detract from the colour of the suite.

If you're short on storage space,
think about swopping your pedestal
basin for a vanity unit — this will give
you a cupboard underneath the basin
and a useful surface surrounding it. Also
try to create a more streamlined and
orderly look by dispensing with clutter
and boxing in unsightly pieces of
plumbing. If you can't box in large pipes,

paint them the same colour as the walls to disguise them. It
may be possible to convert small gaps between fittings into
useful storage space for soaps, towels and shampoo bottles,
otherwise box these in too. A wire basket or nylon storage
pockets on the back of the door can hold soaps, flannels, etc
if you don't have much cupboard space. Or you can invest
in a bath-rack with a mirror attached so everything is to hand
when you're wallowing, and contained when you're not.

If you want more than a
shower but don't have room
for a bath, don't despair.
An extra deep seat bath
could provide the answer to
your problems.

Change your bath taps for one of the new bath-shower
mixers, where the shower flex receedes back into the tap
housing when not in use. In this way you don't have a
tangled flex to contend with when turning on taps.

TILES

Tiles are a must to protect surfaces which come into contact
with water and these days you will find you are spoilt for
choice on the design front. Prices vary enormously, and your
budget will be a deciding factor for what you choose. But it's

A bird's-eye view of a stylish and well designed shower room. Proof that a bathroom isn't always a must for the modern home.

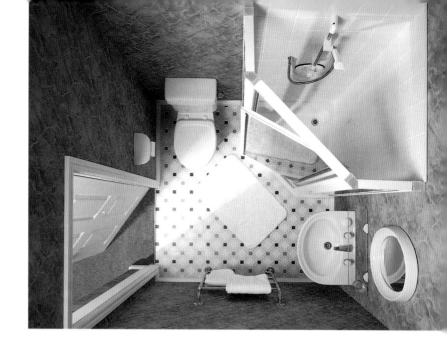

worth bearing in mind that once in place, tiles are not easy to remove and often mean a complete replastering job just to provide a good surface for re-tiling. So make sure you choose a design that you feel sure you can live with for some time, and which really isn't going to put off prospective buyers if you ever come to sell. If in doubt, it's a good idea to stick to a plain colour and add your pattern in the form of flooring, blinds, towels, etc. If you feel all-over tiling looks chilly and institutional, compromise by tiling only around the bath, washbasin and shower, but if you have an over-bath shower mixer, do tile up to the ceiling around it. There's nothing quite like shower spray for making paper peel and paint blister.

FLOORING

The main consideration for bathroom flooring is that it must be waterproof, but you will also want something that looks good and feels comfortable underfoot. There are many options and all have their good and bad points. Carpet is a favourite choice for the comfort element. To combat damp, it's best to choose a rubber-backed type specially designed for bathrooms, although even then it can become a bit smelly in time — especially if there are kids (or an adult) — in the house who splash water around liberally.

Cushioned sheet vinyl is always a good option as it is fairly comfortable underfoot and is usually reasonably priced — but it can be slippery when wet, so be aware of this if there is an elderly or disabled person in the house. Cork tiles have rather fallen from favour recently but they are still a good option for bathrooms, being both warm underfoot and, as long as you choose a sealed range, waterproof too.

Bathrooms which are tiled from floor to ceiling can look very smart, and granite and marble tiles have a real air of luxury about them. But any ceramic flooring will feel cold underfoot and can be dangerously slippery when wet. Make sure you specify that you want non-slip when buying ceramic floor tiles.

LIGHTING

As electricity and water don't mix, it is vital that you have bathroom lighting installed by a professional electrician. Most good bathroom specialists will undertake this work. Alternatively, consult an electrician who is a member of NTCEIC, or a good lighting shop.

Ceiling lights must be enclosed and you could opt for recessed, low-voltage halogen lighting, which is far more effective than a single ceiling fitting and can be controlled to create interesting effects. Three spotlights on a small central unit can direct light into dark corners, highlighting good points and disguising bad ones. Wall lights can be used in the bathroom, but the bulb must be completely enclosed by the shade to protect electrical contacts from steam. In addition, the switch must be a pull cord, away from the light itself.

Small bathrooms are a fact of everyday life for the modern homeowner. But we hope our ideas have proved to you that fitting all the necessary appliances into a room that's restricted both by space and plumbing layout needn't stop you adding a dash of style too. The case study overleaf has many more ideas for you to dwell upon.

---

continued . . .

- *If the space you've got really can't accommodate a bath, don't despair — you can choose a shower instead. If you like to linger at your ablutions, you could have a fold-down shower seat installed.*

- *Unless you are having a fully tiled, walk-in shower room, you will need a cubicle of some type. In this case, a bi-fold or sliding door requires less space for opening than one with a pivot door.*

- *Washbasins and loos are generally pretty standard in size although if you are really tight for room you could consider a small cloakroom basin, some of which are designed to slot into a corner. Alternatively, you could apply a bit of visual trickery to make the sanitaryware appear to take up less room. Wall-hung sanitaryware (no pedestal for the basin, no visable cistern for the loo), keep the floor area free making the bathroom seem more spacious. A wall-hung loo with concealed cistern will also provide you with a useful shelf above it for towels and toiletries. The old-fashioned style of WC with brass piping connecting it to a high-level cistern is another way to make the loo appear to be taking up less room than it is.*

CASE STUDY

This bathroom measures only 1.8 x 2.6m (6 x 8ft 6in), but the limited space has been well planned to provide room for a bath, washbasin, toilet, bidet, and even an airing cupboard.

PRACTICAL POINTERS

There was a lot to fit into this small bathroom — including a central heating boiler — so careful advance planning was essential. The boiler is sited in the left-hand corner and a large airing cupboard built above it. A lift-off tiled panel provides access to the boiler.

Unfortunately, this shortened the 1.8m (6ft) wall under the window which would have been the ideal spot to place the bath. Running the bath along the right-hand wall towards the door was an alternative, but this wouldn't leave enough room for the washbasin. Yet another option was to abandon the bath altogether and install a shower instead, but the owner particularly wanted a bathroom as opposed to a shower room. So, the solution was to install a cast-iron seat bath, which is deeper than average to compensate for its lack of length. It was quite expensive but seemed to provide the perfect answer. It fits neatly into the space and allows the owner to luxuriate when she has the time or use the hand-held shower for a quick freshen-up.

The toilet, washbasin and bidet are all wall-hung models which give an illusion of more space. The cistern is concealed behind a false halfwall, 22.5cms (9ins) out from the main wall, creating extra shelf spae for towels and accessories. All taps and accessories are white to maintain a streamlined look — too many coloured accessories would just look cluttered.

DECORATIVE DETAILS

The tile colours were chosen first — a soft, pale aqua for both walls and floor helps to keep the room as light as possible. The floor tiles are non-slip, an important consideration in wet areas such as bathrooms and kitchens. A paint colour was matched to the aqua tiles, and mint green and a darker blue were added as accent colours for border tiles and matching towels. By painting the airing cupboard the same blue as the walls and using a concealed magnetic catch instead of a handle, it blends into the background.

Reeded glass gives privacy but still admits light, and instead of a plain bath panel, semi-rounded dowel was used to echo the lines of the glass. The vertical lines also help to disguise a small cupboard built underneath the bath to store cleaning equipment. The window recess is fitted with glass shelves which display a collection of coloured glass, but could equally hold perfume bottles and toiletries.

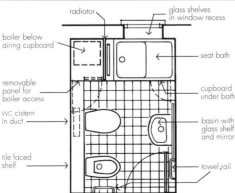

radiator

glass shelves in window recess

boiler below airing cupboard

seat bath

removable panel for boiler access

cupboard under bath

WC cistern in duct

basin with glass shelf and mirror

tile faced shelf

towel rail

AT A GLANCE

- Wall-hung toilet, bidet and wash basin create an impression of space by keeping the floor area free.

- The loo cistern is concealed behind a false half wall for neatness, and creates a 22.5-cm (9-in) wide shelf for towels and accessories.

- A space-saving seat-bath measures 1050mm long x 700mm wide x 760mm deep. Its extra depth makes up for the shorter length.

- A stylish towel-radiator heats the bathroom and keeps towels warm and dry. It can be supplied with an electric immersion heater making it independent of the heating system in summer. It is available in several sizes.

- The under-bath space is utilized as storage for cleaning equipment etc, with pull-out wire baskets on runners.

- The airing cupboard door has a magnetic catch instead of a handle to look unobtrusive.

- Taps and towel rails are white to blend with sanitary ware and create a cleaner look.

THE SMALLEST ROOM

The loo, lavatory, WC, little girl's room — whatever it's called in your house, it can prove difficult to decorate. As a purely functional area, it doesn't really merit top priority on the decorating schedule. But — along with the sitting room — it's the place your guests are most likely to visit, so if you want to make a good impression, brush up on small space style.

There is no doubt that an extra loo in the house has many advantages. Cutting down on the early morning queue will be a boon in any family home, as will no longer finding yourself stranded outside a locked bathroom door while a guest wallows contentedly, oblivious to your distress! Furthermore, estate agents claim, two loos are always a good selling point. So if you're not already a two loo family, it's worth exploring the possibility of hiving off some space from elsewhere in the home to install an extra WC.

This is relatively easy where you have an area on an outside wall which can be plumbed into the main soil stack. The space under the stairs, an old larder or coal-hole are the most common areas which are made use of, but if you really don't have any redundant space, then it may be worth having a small extension built on the back of the house. However you approach it, it's best to seek expert plumbing advice before you start. Then, having decided on the suitability of your site, the first items to choose will be the WC and washbasin.

Fittings

These days, the WC comes in a bewildering range of styles and colours. Manufacturers have surpassed themselves in making a fashion element out of an item which only two generations ago had no place in many houses at all — it was kept out in the back garden.

Now we can choose from high-level, low-level and concealed cisterns. We can make our selection from dozens of different shaped bowls, in almost any colour from 'Pampas' to 'Aqua'. We even have the dilemma of which kind of seat to go for — hard wood, soft wood, plastic or painted. Aside from allowing ourselves a wry smile at the very irony of this situation, we should also make the most of it to get what we want to suit our particular requirements.

The designs you go for will depend largely on whether you want to establish a contemporary or traditional look. Nostalgia has been the driving force for design in the home over the last seven or eight years — and nowhere more-so than in the loo and bathroom. Of course, we don't wish to return to the basic workings of these antique models. Rather, we want the combination of modern plumbing, with the looks of the originals. So, replicas of Victorian high-level cisterns with pull chains and long brass tubing have become a feature of many contemporary homes, along with washbasins and lavatory bowls decorated with elegant twining floral patterns and dark wooden mahogany seats.

If you prefer something more modern in design, there are now concealed low-level cisterns which are hidden behind a panel on the wall and give the whole thing a more streamlined effect.

If you are stuck with an existing low-level cistern which for one reason or another is rather uninspiring, you can box it in. You will obviously need to be able to reposition the flush handle or build around it, and you will need too, to provide access to the cistern in case of any malfunction. This is easy enough; simply attach the top of the panelling with screws which can be undone if necessary. If you take the panelling right down to the floor, you can incorporate a small cupboard either side for storage.

THE WASHBASIN

Washbasins come in many shapes and sizes, with some being specifically designed for use in loos and cloakrooms.

Midnight blue and touches of gold give this loo an exotic touch and prove that short on space doesn't have to mean short on style.

An old printer's type case full of miniature collectables provides a distraction for visitors to this WC.

With either a flat back, an angled edge to fit in a corner, or a semi-recessed design, you should be able to find a model to suit most situations, however cramped.

To cater for those with a love of nostalgia, there are antiqued pine units which look for all the world like an old washstand, but instead of sporting the traditional china jug and bowl, the top has an inset basin with taps and a plug and waste. The plumbing is neatly concealed within the base unit, which also has a cupboard for storage of toiletries and cleaning materials.

Decorative details

As well as being the smallest room in the house, the loo often has the added problem of being an awkward shape, making it difficult to work in when you start to paint and wallpaper. You are fairly limited too by what will actually fit in this limited space.

Aside from the necessities, some kind of cupboard (in which to hide away loo rolls, and cleaning materials), and in some instances a small table or chair, are about the only extra pieces of furniture you will have room for. So interest has to be created by what you choose to put on the walls, at the window and on the floor. The one advantage when decorating the loo is that it should be fairly inexpensive as you won't need much of the materials you choose.

We are not really concerned in this instance with attempting to make the room appear larger. After all, it is somewhere that you occupy for only short periods of time, so all that is really required is to be able to get to and from the loo and washbasin without getting cramp or claustrophobia.

Wallpaper or paint are equally suitable choices for walls, or you may prefer to use ceramic tiles. It certainly makes sense to tile a splashback above the basin and possibly around the loo. In such a small area, however, you should avoid the whole thing looking bitty, so it's best to stick to one or two colours and limit the amount of pattern. To make cleaning easier, choose a vinyl wallcovering or a vinyl silk emulsion paint which can be washed or wiped clean.

FLOORING

This should ideally be resistant to damp and easy to keep clean — for this reason carpet is never a very good choice. Vinyl flooring is the most obvious option and comes in a wide variety of colours and patterns. Linoleum too is a possibility. It has shaken off its dated image as a flooring of the 1950s and is appearing again in many homes because it wears very well and also because it can be cut and laid into many different designs. A chequerboard effect with two colours or a single colour with a contrasting border are both simple designs which can add a touch of sophistication without looking too fussy in a small space.

It may be small, but this loo will definitely encourage you to look on the bright side of life. Notice the novel way in which reading matter is provided!

WINDOWS

What to put at the window is always a difficult choice as you obviously want privacy, but also want to let as much light in as possible. The usual solution is frosted glass and there is now a mass of new variations on the frosted glass theme.

Another thought is etched glass. A revival of the method used to glaze many Victorian and Edwardian doors, a design or pattern is etched with acid into the glass and the whole surface has a very fine textural finish which admits light in but is otherwise opaque — even at night. Inevitably though, it also prevents you from seeing out, so if your loo window happens to have a breathtaking view and you are not

overlooked, then it may not be the right choice. There are ranges of off-the-peg designs to choose from — both modern and traditional — or there are companies who will custom design for you if you want a particular design or image. Etched glass is, incidentally, also an ideal choice for the door to a loo if you want it to be part glazed. If the loo window is small and natural light limited, a part glazed door off a lighter hallway will help the situation.

Finally, before leaving the subject of decorative glass, you many not have thought of stained glass. Once only seen in church windows, there are now many craftspeople who produce stained glass for domestic situations. It can be fashioned in both traditional and very modern designs and creates a beautiful effect with sunlight streaming through it — a decorative touch which could become the focal point of the whole room.

You can, of course, have curtains — the fabric will have a softening effect on the whole room — but where a window is particularly small, they always look a bit unnecessary and it's probably preferable to have a blind of some sort. Austrian blinds (or 'Knicker blinds' as they have become known in some circles!) are still very popular and will work at quite a small window although they do look very frilly and fussy, so are only right for a very feminine style of room. Roman blinds are much neater and better for a more formal look. If you want a window dressing which will cover the window all the time, then fine-slat Venetian blinds are a good idea. The slats can be angled to allow plenty of light in but retain privacy too.

THE FINISHING TOUCHES

In terms of the colours or patterns you choose, the world is really your oyster. You can be fairly restrained or you could go totally over the top. For although we 'furnish' the loo in accordance with its purpose, once the basics are installed there's no harm in having a bit of fun with the decoration. Because the colour scheme doesn't have to become such a major issue as that for a sitting room or kitchen, if mistakes are made it isn't too much of a problem and the room is small enough to have another attempt at getting it right.

Here are a few creative ideas we have seen work very well: a seaside theme, in blues and greens with colourful fish fixed on the wall and a shell-trimmed mirror; a tiny loo decked out like the inside of a brightly coloured tent, with striped wallpaper on the walls and laid diagonally to a point on the centre of the ceiling, and a very sophisticated design based on the idea of a print room, with photocopies of old engravings surrounded by photocopied decorative borders, swags and bows.

To place reading matter in the loo has become almost standard practice — compilations of cartoons, famous people's memoirs or, the height of ridiculousness, a weighty volume of *War and Peace*, are all guaranteed to keep visitors occupied or at least to raise a smile. Pictures will help too — why not create a mini gallery? Amusing photographs of family and friends, a collection of your favourite cartoons, cut out of the paper and framed, or even a couple of favourite prints or paintings — these are all ways to jolly up your loo and prove that the best things really do come in small packages.

A mix of three different wallpapers and two borders are successfully used together in this very small space because they have a common colour and design theme. The wallpaper on the shutters is a clever idea and creates an unusual focal point.

CASE STUDY

Although the slightly odd angles and classic blue and white decoration give this loo a pretty, cottagey look, it has actually been created under the stairs in a suburban house.

PRACTICAL POINTERS

Cleverly designed to make full use of the otherwise redundant space below the stairs, this tiny loo was created with the children of the house in mind. This not only means that the main bathroom is now left in some semblance of order, but it has helped alleviate the morning rush-hour queues. The miniature washbasin is specially designed to fit into small spaces and ideal for this situation. It is sited at a lower height than normal, for use by the children, and an integral splash-back makes it easier to clean. If your basin is sited at standard height, young children can be elevated by using a plastic step-up until they grow taller.

Flooring in the loo should ideally be waterproof and easy to keep clean. The one shown here is designed to look like stripped wood painted with a coloured stain, but is, in fact, synthetic with a water-resistant finish.

Lighting is provided by a single wall light, mounted above the mirror. Although its style is not really in keeping with the cottage look, it does give a good amount of light and the glass globe completely encloses the bulb, which is always a wise precaution in a room where water is in use.

DECORATIVE DETAILS

The colour combination of blue and white is a classic one that always looks good, and you can successfully mix several patterns so long as you stick with roughly the same shade of blue throughout. Here a wallpaper and border patterned with shells are mixed with floral tiles and curtains. Blue and white Chinese ceramics provide the perfect finishing touch for a fresh, cottagey look.

The sanitaryware in this loo is plain white, but among the many reproductions of Victorian designs available these days are WCs and cisterns patterned with blue flowers — so you could splash out and have a blue and white loo too!

Mirror, loo seat and matching accessories in a dark mahogany stain have been chosen here, although pine would look just as good.

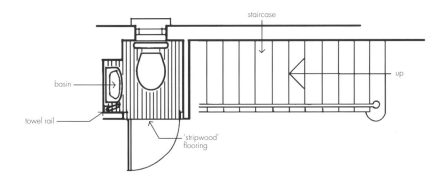

AT A GLANCE

• This tiny loo makes the most of what would otherwise be redundant space under the stairs.

• As there are young children in the house, the washbasin has been sited at a lower height than normal.

• The miniature basin has an integral splashback and is ideal for small spaces.

• The colour combination of blue and white is a classic choice. And keeping to the same colour theme means you can mix several patterns with great success.

• A narrow border patterned with shells is used at ceiling height, around the tiled splashback and again as detail between the loo and window sill.

• A synthetic flooring combines the effect of stripped wood flooring with the practicality of a waterproof surface — vital for a loo which is used primarily by children.

NURSERY

If a new baby means turning a tiny bedroom into a nursery, don't worry — with a little careful planning you can create somewhere even the most discerning of infants will be proud to call home.

The most surprising aspect of a new addition to the family is the incredible amount of paraphernalia that seems to surround such a tiny creature. That's why the first rule of the game is to learn to be ruthless about what is really necessary and what you can do without. When space is at a premium you can't afford to make mistakes.

So start by making a list of the real essentials for any nursery: somewhere for the baby to sleep, somewhere to store all its things and a place for changing it. Everything else is an extra. For instance, you don't need a baby bath on a stand, which takes up masses of room. You'd do better to choose one that you can use in your own bath (some parents even get away with a washing-up bowl at first).

Decorative details

Before you start designing and furnishing the room, consider your own future plans. If you're going to be looking for a bigger place soon, then you will want to buy things you can take with you — and that goes for decoration too. Not all would-be buyers will be won over by strong nursery prints or Batman all over the walls, whereas curtains and cot covers can be easily taken with you.

Storage for toys is a must for any child's room. One idea is a toy chest such as this one which has been painted and stencilled to match the room.

Colours are a matter of personal taste although pastels seem right for a baby's room somehow — and when the room is small, pale colours will also help to make it seem more spacious. Walls can be papered or painted and it's fun to have an excuse to use some of the lovely nursery designs which are available these days. If your budget is tight, plain painted walls can be jollied up with a wallpaper border or stencil. There are so many different images to choose from, and plenty which are designed especially for children. It is easy to paint over these with a slightly more grown-up design as the baby gets older.

When it comes to choosing flooring for a nursery, carpet is probably the best choice as you will want something which is warm and comfortable underfoot for those night-time mercy missions, and if the room is quite small, this shouldn't be too expensive. Alternatively, a cushioned vinyl might prove more practical if the child is to remain in this room when it gets older. In the meantime, you could add a rug to warm it up a bit — cotton rag rugs are cheap and can be machine-washed. Don't forget to attach an anti-slip pad underneath to avoid accidents. You can buy this by the metre and cut it to size.

Lighting is a most important consideration in children's rooms in order to make them feel happy and secure at bedtime. A night-light will lend a gentle glow to the room through the night and prevent you from stubbing toes if you have to attend any distress calls. It's possible to buy light fittings in the shape of animals or fluffy toys and ones which combine with a mobile too. Put your central light on a dimmer switch, particularly if you don't have a night-light. If you intend to adapt the room as the child grows, plan ahead by making sure there are plenty of suitably positioned electric sockets for extra lighting, computers, stereo etc. These should, of course, be fitted with safety covers while children are still very young.

This baby-changing unit stores all the vital accoutrements underneath, hidden by a cotton curtain. As the baby grows older, the curtain can be removed and the unit adapted to hold books and toys.

Furniture

However attractive, a crib isn't really necessary — and it has a limited lifespan of only four to five months. If you can't resist one, then pick a design that folds up for easy space-saving storage later. Instead, it is much better to design your room around the one item you will definitely need for at least two years: a proper cot. There's no reason why a baby shouldn't go straight into a full-size cot provided you wrap him or her securely. Alternatively, you could use a carry cot at first.

When space is so important, it pays to choose a cot that comes with a storage drawer underneath. Alternatively, a lot of the cots on sale now can be converted to a small bed when the child is older, but whether you opt for this or not depends on whether you plan to have more than one baby. Also, if you will be moving in the meantime, baby number one may end up with a room big enough for the size of bed not to be a problem. A chest of drawers is more useful than a wardrobe, as babies' clothes tend to be folded rather than hung and it also takes up less space. But it isn't worth buying special scaled-down baby designs, as these soon outlive their usefulness. It's easy to prettify the more traditional chests with stencils and transfers, and the size won't really make that much difference.

If you do want to hang up some items, a clotheshorse is a better bet. It takes up little room and is easily portable too. A dado rail is especially practical for a baby's room — it means you can attach stick-on hooks for displaying baby clothes, which these days are often too pretty to hide away. These can be removed when the baby gets older. An Anaglypta paper — nursery ranges are now available — is a good idea for the lower half of the wall which will all too soon become vulnerable to sticky little fingers.

BUILT-IN FURNITURE

Built-in furniture can save space, of course, but it is only really worth considering if you plan to stay put for a while, in which case it can be designed to adapt as your child grows older. For instance, a worktop that you use for changing a baby now could turn out to be perfect for housing a junior computer later on.

There are specialist firms who will turn fitted cupboards into something really special — with drawers that look like car bumpers, a favourite animal or a little house. But such designs are expensive and although they make the most of the space, you need to be sure you get your money's worth from them — they won't necessarily be a selling point. If you do go for fitted cupboards, it pays — in terms of space — to leave an alcove for the cot that will also be large enough to take a proper bed. Useful ceiling-height cupboards can be built over the top of it, so you won't actually loose on space.

SOMEWHERE FOR CHANGING

Special changing stands usually have a few useful drawers as well as a PVC changing pad. Although these are convenient, they take up a lot of space, so if you buy one choose a design that could be used as something else later. For instance, some are built in the form of cubes that dismantle and can be used separately for storage or even as a bedside table. But provided your choice of chest of drawers is high enough for you to bend over without too much trouble, you can simply put a changing mat on top of it. Some chests are specially designed for this, with a ridge around the top to hold the mat in place while you change the baby.

SPACE SAVERS

● *It pays to make the most of the walls. Rows of flat-backed baskets in pretty pastel colours (really designed to take dried flowers) look good in a nursery and can be cleverly arranged to hold toiletries and bits and bobs.*

● *Hanging pockets are also useful, and particularly good to use on the back of a door.*

● *Use specially designed nursery zipper bags to hang up spare bedding.*

● *If you have the right shape window, build in a window seat which can be used as a toy box too. But remember that it will also give easy access to the window, so fix safety bars.*

CASE STUDY

The charm of this delightful baby's room, measuring 1.8 x 2.4m (6 x 8 ft), is the number of imaginative and versatile ideas which have been incorporated into such a small space.

PRACTICAL POINTERS

For best use of the limited space, the main items — a cot and cupboards — were built in. The cot is fairly easy for a competent DIY-er to make, but remember that it should conform to British Safety Standards. The relevant guidelines pamphlet is number 1753. Look for a copy at your local library, or contact the British Standards Authority on 0908 221166.

By raising the cot 30 cms (1ft) off the floor enough room was created for drawers underneath. For ease of movement, these are on castors, and the drawer interiors are wipe-clean melamine. Whale-shaped handles are a fun touch. These were cut out of ¼-in MDF, using a fretsaw, and then painted.

Although all the items to be stored in a baby's room are miniature, there are still plenty of them, so some well-organized storage was a must. Floor-to-ceiling cupboards were built in next to the cot. They currently contain shelves for clothes and linen but some of the shelves can be replaced with a hanging rail as the baby grows.

The free-standing changing unit is home-made too, although you can buy similar ready-made designs. This particular unit has the advantage of being adaptable. Once

the curtain is removed, it will become a simple shelving unit which can store books and toys for an older child.

DECORATIVE DETAILS

Stencilling has been used to great effect in this pretty room, with stars covering the white-painted walls and rows of yachts sailing around the room at dado height. Stencilled onto a yellow background and enclosed with lengths of wooden beading, the yachts form a pretty border. Even the cupboard fronts have been enlivened with an alphabet and a seahorse design.

Walls can be papered or painted and it's fun to have an excuse to use some of the lovely nursery designs which are available these days. If your budget is tight, plain painted walls can be jollied up with a wallpaper border or stencil. There are a great many different images to choose from, and plenty which are designed especially for children. It is easy to paint over these with a more grown-up design as your baby gets older.

When it comes to choosing flooring for a nursery, carpet is probably the best choice as you will want something which is warm and comfortable underfoot for those night-time mercy missions, and if the room is quite small, this shouldn't be too expensive. Alternatively, a cushioned vinyl might prove more practical if the child is to remain in this room when it gets older. In the meantime, you could add a rug to warm it up a bit — cotton rag rugs are cheap and can be machine-washed. Don't forget to

attach an anti-slip pad beneath it to avoid accidents. You can buy this by the metre and cut it to size.

Lighting is a most important consideration in children's rooms to help them feel happy and secure at bedtime. A night-light will lend a gentle glow to the room through the night and prevent you from stubbing toes if you have to attend any distress calls. And babies' rooms are one area where a central ceiling pendant is a positively good idea. As they will be lying on their backs much of the time, whatever amusement or distractions you can offer will be helpful. It's possible to buy light fittings in the shape of animals or fluffy toys and ones which combine with a mobile too. Put your central light on a dimmer switch, particularly if you don't have a night light. If the room is to adapt as the child grows, plan ahead by making sure there are plenty of suitably positioned electric sockets for extra lighting, computers, stereo, etc. These should, of course, be fitted with safety covers while children are still very young.

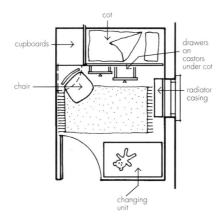

AT A GLANCE

- Cot and cupboards have been specially made to fit into the limited space along the back wall.

- Built-in drawers underneath the cot are perfect for storing toys and pull out on castors for easy access.

- Stencilling is used as an inexpensive alternative to wallpaper and border.

- A radiator cover looks decorative, protects probing fingers and provides vents over which to air linens too.

- Cork covered with fabric and ribbon makes a simple pin-board.

- Curtains are lined with a contrasting fabric and trimmed with binding. A length of binding threaded through the metal eyelets is an easy and unusual way to hang curtains.

- The curtains are held back with patches of Velcro and tiny wooden starfish.

CHILDREN'S ROOM

A child's bedroom may have to be a playroom, study and retreat as well as somewhere to rest a weary head. It is also likely to be theirs for some years, perhaps until they leave home. Creating a room which is flexible enough to fulfil a number of requirements can be quite a challenge — especially if you are short on space to begin with.

Decorative details

When decorating children's rooms, it's important to take their views into account, but the design you choose should be adaptable enough to allow for changes in their tastes, needs and lifestyle. Bear in mind too, how long you plan to be in your present home — this is bound to affect the amount of money you are prepared to spend.

Don't fall into the trap of decorating from top to bottom with a themed design — Thomas the Tank Engine and My Little Pony are the current favourites. A five-year-old might love it, but his or her taste is sure to change in a couple of years and you will then have an expensive redecorating job on your hands. If you really can't divert your child from one of these designs, then give way on one item such as the bedlinen which will need replacing after a few years anyway, and stick to something plainer and more adaptable for wallcoverings, flooring and curtains.

If children are sharing a room you will probably find it quite difficult to cater for their different ages and interests. In this case, you may have to compromise on decoration, and planning will be even more crucial. If possible, give them each an area to call their own and for which they are responsible. A set of freestanding shelves can help to create a partition, to delineate one area from another.

WALLS

Vertical stripes or a small subtle pattern are a good option if you want wallpaper as they won't date and need only be replaced when worn out. They will also make the most of a small room and allow the emphasis to be placed on toys, mobiles and pictures. It's also a good idea to choose a wallcovering with a vinyl finish which is hard-wearing and

The lack of space and quirky shape of this child's room actually add to its charm. And there is a definite feel of the doll's house about the way it is furnished and decorated.

can be wiped clean or washed when necessary. Plain, painted walls are a good basis for cheap and flexible decoration as they can be livened up with a wallpaper border, or perhaps some stencilling which are easy to change as you or the child tires of them.

A large pinboard is a must for children of all ages. It will provide a surface for displaying early schoolwork, drawings, postcards and the inevitable pop or pony posters, preventing walls from being marked with tape or drawing pins.

Some children can't resist scribbling on walls. One solution is to fit a dado rail and hang wipe-clean plastic or PVC below it while your child is quite young. This should prevent any further damage — and you can still paper above the dado.

This stylish teenage room
has been adapted as its
occupant has grown up. The
basic framework has
remained the same but has
been repainted and files
and books have replaced
the toys which used to fill the
shelves.

FLOORING

The main criteria when choosing any flooring, and
particularly for a child's room, are comfort, warmth, and
ease of cleaning. If the room is used solely for sleeping, ie if
you have a separate play room, then carpet is the obvious
choice. It is less practical, however, if this is a room for

activity as well as a bedroom. The best option in this case is
carpet tiles. They are usually synthetic and therefore easy to
clean, and if any marks prove indelible, you can dispose of
the offending tiles and replace them with a couple of new
ones. Indeed, it might be wise to buy a few extra tiles at the
time of purchase.

SPACE SAVERS

A tidy room is one of the best ways to create an illusion of space. To help teach children to clear up clutter, storage must be accessible and attractive.

● *Open shelving is versatile enough to house anything from toys and books to clothing and can often be painted to co-ordinate with the room. The drawback is that nothing can be hidden away — but then again you might use this in an attempt to encourage tidiness!*

● *Coat hooks and peg boards fixed at a suitably low height are ideal for hanging anything from small pairs of lace-up shoes to hats and scarves.*

● *A great method for 'hideaway' storage is a bed with built-in drawers beneath. These are usually large enough to store everything from toys and clothes to spare bedlinen and have the added advantage of preventing children from 'tidying' things away under the bed.*

● *Alternatively, double up storage with seating. A large toy chest can be made from a pine blanket box — painted and stencilled in jolly colours. Or buy small benches which have hinged seats and storage space inside.*

The only other real option is a vinyl flooring which can be scrubbed clean, is still fairly warm underfoot and comes in a wide choice of patterns and designs. It can, however, look a bit utilitarian in a bedroom.

Furniture

Adaptability is the key word when furnishing a child's room — you need to select items which will grow with the child. One of the easiest ways to do this, and to save space, is to buy a complete bed unit that incorporates both play and work areas, and sometimes even cupboard space and shelving. These can usually have the configuration changed around as your child develops new interests and activities.

BEDS

Bunk beds which can be dismantled to form two separate beds when the children are older are a good idea. Some models will adapt to form a 'L' shape which has more potential for children at an intermediate stage. It is also worth thinking ahead to how you might use the room once a child has left home. You may want to turn the room into a guest room or study. So when you are choosing the original furniture, always consider the extent of its adaptability for later use.

For older children, a platform bed creates an interesting arrangement and will enable the space directly underneath to be used as a study or hobby area. For safety's sake, however, this design should not be considered if you have very young children. If in any doubt about the safety of bunk or platform beds, consult British Standards Authority pamphlet BS 6998 at your local library or by telephoning 0908 221166 before you buy.

Children love the idea of having a friend to stay. If you don't have the space for more than one bed, you can get round the problem by buying a single bed with a pull-out drawer underneath which is actually a spare bed. When not in use, the 'guest' bed simply slides back underneath. There are also small versions of that classic space-saver — the sofa-bed. Made from cubes of foam covered in fun patterns, the chairs unfold to provide the perfect place for an extra weary head!

LIGHTING

As with other areas of the home, it helps to have a mix of lighting for children's room. The main light source will be either a ceiling pendant or wall lights and it should be on a dimmer switch which will help a young child gradually get used to the dark, or it can be supplemented with a small night light. For younger children, jolly up the ceiling pendant with an imaginative lampshade — there are designs which incorporate a mobile or fluffy toy. You can replace this with a more sophisticated design when the child is older. An innovative idea which kids will love are luminous wallpapers and borders which will keep children entertained even after lights out.

Once homework and hobbies become a consideration, an angelpoise lamp is a good idea. These are relatively inexpensive, are available in bright colours and will fix onto a desk or bed-end.

Problems can arise if children who share a room have different bedtimes. A light that fits onto the headboard or a mini-clip light which clips onto a book will let an older child have some extra reading time without disturbing the younger one.

As children get older their own taste can gradually be incorporated into the room by using lampshades, bedlinen or rugs to add splashes of a favourite colour or design. And the point will eventually come when your taste is irrelevant. You might be asked for advice, you will certainly be expected to cough up for the cost, but your child's room will become his or her haven, full of their things.

continued . . .

● *Colourful plastic or wooden boxes appeal to children and are the cheapest, brightest and easiest way of clearing clutter when bedtime comes around. As an even cheaper alternative, cover cardboard boxes with coloured paper or PVC.*

● *Bags with compartment pockets designed for holding shoes can be put to good use for storing small toys. They can be hung up behind the door when full, or rolled up out of the way when not in use.*

● *Children sharing a room will be encouraged to keep it tidy if they have their own storage space. Try colour-coding drawers, pinboards and boxes or allocating separate shelves.*

This delightful children's room mixes coordinated soft furnishings with specially designed and painted furniture to create a perfect little playroom-cum-bedroom.

PRACTICAL POINTERS

This delightful room is both playroom and bedroom to its little occupant so there is plenty of storage space for tidying toys away when bedtime comes. The painted bench has a hinged seat which lifts up to store larger toys, while the jumbo doll's house in the corner is a novel idea for putting smaller bits and pieces behind closed doors. The sentry box is, in fact, a wardrobe which is quite large enough to store clothes for a young child.

All the furniture is made from MDF. It is easy to cut, provides a smooth surface for painting and is sturdy and robust, and so ideal for children's furniture.

The fabric and wallcoverings are from a range designed especially for children so they are not too babyish. In this way, they won't need replacing in a couple of years time.

Although the choice of carpet may be slightly impractical for a child's room, it is warm and comfortable and at least the colour shouldn't show the dirt too easily. Other options would have been a cushioned vinyl or cork which are still reasonably comfortable but easier to keep clean.

DECORATIVE DETAILS

The whole room is a clever mix of colours which although they are in a child's room actually look quite

sophisticated. As the fabrics and wallcoverings are all from the same collection they work well together, and several of the colours have been picked out for the painted furniture.

The table and bench have both been given a combed finish using two paint colours. A pale blue was painted on as a solid base coat. When dry, the darker blue was

applied on top and a rubber comb —
available from specialist suppliers —
is dragged through the wet paint
lifting some of the top colour off in
order to show the paler shade lying
underneath.

The sentry box, which is also a
wardrobe, was given a similar
treatment to create the woodgrain
effect.

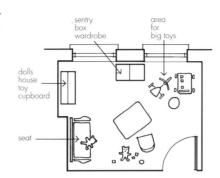

AT A GLANCE

- A range of coordinated wallpapers and fabrics ensures all the colours work together and then individual touches are added in the form of specially designed, painted furniture.

- The furnishings don't look too 'babyish' and so will still look good for a few years yet as the child is growing up.

- Unusual storage is provided by the hinged seat on the bench, a jumbo-sized doll's house and a sentry box which is, in fact, a wardrobe.

- A pretty Edwardian folding beach chair has had a new seat added — in a nursery fabric — making it ideal for use in a child's room.

- The furniture is made from MDF which is easy to cut into decorative shapes, has a smooth surface for painting and is robust enough for use in children's rooms.

TEENAGE DEN

With a bit of planning, even a tiny boxroom can be turned into a place for teenagers to entertain their friends without the rest of you having to know too much about it.

For a successful den there must be a 'no adults' rule. So make it clear from the start that you expect the place to be kept clean and tidy without you. Buy a decent-sized rubbish bin and make it a rule that it's emptied regularly. A brightly coloured dustbin can be the answer — and is useful for storage too.

A kettle in the room means you're less likely to have hordes descending on your kitchen. Try to incorporate somewhere specially for drinks if you can, then you won't have to spend hours mopping up spilt coke. Even if your kids are into the fad for personal organizers, few of them ever refer to them, so a notice board that can take an at-a-glance diary is important. It will also give you somewhere to pin messages — for as anyone with teenagers knows, notes are often your only form of regular contact.

Whether you allow a phone in the room is up to you. It does mean the rest of you are spared hours of listening to endless droning from the hall, but make sure they are only incoming calls by installing a special lock on that extension. They are relatively cheap and are available from some mail order catalogues. If phone bills are a problem, you could consider a separate line altogether. Try the payphone sort or one which doesn't let the user make outgoing calls. Installation costs may put you off, but in the long term it can be a good idea — especially if the phone-loving teenager helps towards the cost.

Decorative details

All of us have ideas of what we think teenagers like. In fact, they often tend to be a surprisingly conventional lot, so before you reach for the acid-green paint it's as well to discuss plans carefully. It's important not to impose your ideas for decoration if they are to be encouraged to use the room and think of it as their own.

A camp-bed is a must for teenagers who have friends to stay. This one folds up into a cylindrical bag which can be stored in a cupboard or under the bed.

You might like to think that with older kids you no longer have to worry about sticky fingers, but remember that their visitors may not be so bothered about damage to the walls, so it's not a bad idea to put in a dado rail and use a painted relief-patterned paper on the bottom half.

Furniture

Floor cushions always go down well and any sort of built-in seating is useful — especially if it's designed to hold storage space too — make use of alcoves or bay windows for this if you can. The units needn't be that deep, and shelves with slots for records and tapes can be incorporated into the design. Folding chairs can hang on wall racks or be stored away in cupboards when not in use.

Noise is always a problem — music just isn't worth listening to unless it's loud. So if you can, site the den on the side of the house where there isn't an adjoining wall with next door. Try to make it the back of the house, too, or passers-by will think you're having a party every night. Headphones are essential too.

A stripped floor may look nice, but it's very noisy — teenagers have that way of walking that makes the whole house shake. Practicality may dictate that you choose linoleum, but if your kids aren't too accident-prone with spills and so on, it's worth considering carpet — the thicker the better. If you go for a tough man-made sort it shouldn't break the bank. Carpet tiles are another good option as you can replace any which become badly damaged or stained.

If funds can stretch to it, a computer for games, a TV — to use as a monitor as well as to watch — and a video will be all the equipment needed to keep teenagers relatively quiet for hours. Hiring a TV with video can be reasonably inexpensive and payments can usually be coped with from the proceeds of a paper round — something well worth encouraging.

You will also need to think about homework. For real concentration, a worktop somewhere well away from the

This teenage room has been carefully designed to suit its shape and size. Shelves are built into the alcove, a long worksurface runs around the walls and the recess in the chimney breast is used to site the ubiquitous computer.

television, such as in the bedroom, is a good idea. Nevertheless, try to incorporate a well-lit area in the den for art projects, writing up notes and even the odd letter. A pull-down flap is space-saving and if you can site it so that the teenager has his or her back to the TV it's even better.

In a traditional three-bedroom house with the average family of four, space will be at a premium. But if you have two boys or two girls it can be a good idea to have one bedroom for sleeping and the other as a proper den. However, if your den has to cater for sleeping too, the first step is to find a sofa-bed strong enough to be used every day. And pick one with built-in storage if you can. Alternatively, you could consider a bed that is wall hung and can be pulled down at night. Or there are others that come in a 'cupboard' and can be shut away for the daytime.

All in all, if you've got a spare room it pays to give teenagers their own place — at least they can then feel comfortable about bringing friends home and you have the peace of mind of knowing where they are and (to a certain extent) what they're doing.

Lack of space isn't a problem in this tiny box room. Bright colours and clever storage ideas have turned it into the perfect teenage den.

PRACTICAL POINTERS

Plenty of storage space is vital to help keep a small room such as this free of teenager's clutter. So floor-to-ceiling cupboards with shelves and hanging space to store clothes, books and sports gear have been installed here. Although the cupboards run the whole length of one wall, they are quite shallow to avoid using up too much of the limited floor area. The bi-fold doors are ideal for tight

corners and wherever it would be impossible to open conventional cupboard doors.

More storage is provided underneath a bench on the window wall. Sturdy benches are also good for seating and they can be supplemented by floor cushions and folding chairs.

Folding furniture is, of course, essential in a room this size. The main table is made from a pair of trestles with a piece of wood cut to size for the top. There is also a simple fold-up flap under the window which gives an extra surface and can be folded down against the wall when not in use. A painted wooden wall rack looks good as well as being infinitely practical for hanging up everything from bags to folding chairs.

DECORATIVE DETAILS

All the paintwork is vinyl matt emulsion which will wipe clean and is fairly easy to touch up in the event of any knocks or dents.

For flooring, vinyl tiles which are easy to sweep or wipe clean and are pretty hardwearing, are probably the best surface in a room such as this. They have the added benefit that if any of them do become damaged they can easily be replaced.

Brightly painted shutters are a fun choice for the windows in a teenager's room and instead of any fixed upholstery, use cushions to soften the bench seats. Lighting should be a mix of good general light and task-lighting — especially if this is to be a place for reading and doing homework as well as watching television.

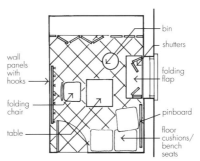

AT A GLANCE

• Floor-to-ceiling cupboards provide plenty of storage space but are quite shallow to avoid using up too much vital floor area. Folding doors open easily in a limited space.

• A painted wooden wall rack looks good and keeps bags, jackets and even folding chairs off the floor.

• Brightly coloured cushions can be removed for washing, and soften up practical bench seats.

• A camp bed for overnight guests is stored folded up in the cupboards.

• Vinyl floor tiles laid in a checkerboard pattern look lively and are easy to keep clean too.

• Trestles and a piece of painted wood form a simple table which can be stored away when not in use. An extra flap-down surface under the window is a piece of MDF.

• A slimline radiator works well — and looks 'cool'.

STUDIO FLAT

Forget the limitations for a moment and look on the bright side. Small flats are inexpensive to heat, take less time to clean, and if well planned can offer you a compact and labour-saving home.

Living in a box doesn't mean that there's no room for creative ideas. In fact, studios need even more imaginative planning. Everything from the colours you paint it to how you organize your storage needs to be carefully thought out and there are dozens of design ideas you can employ to make your small home seem larger.

In studio flats the layout has usually been predetermined, either during its construction or conversion, so your options for the layout may be fairly limited. But basically you will need to cook, eat, wash, sleep — and perhaps serve up the occasional meal for friends — all in this miniature home, so how you organize your space is pretty vital.

Kitchen

The most effective way to delineate the kitchen from the rest of the room is by building a breakfast bar of some type. This will not only give you a place to eat, but can also be used as a workspace when preparing food and can have cupboard space incorporated underneath for storage. Finding ways to keep your worksurfaces clear is important, so the more storage space the better.

The items which will take up worksurface space are a sink and possibly a hob. Circular sinks come in a variety of finishes and will take up less room than a conventional sink and drainer. For draining dishes you could put up an upright drainer which hangs on a wall or a wooden plate rack which looks decorative too.

WORKTOPS

As there won't be a draining area by your sink, the worksurface should be made from a waterproof material. Ceramic tiles, marble, granite or slate are all options, as is waxed or varnished wood. All have their advantages and disadvantages. Ceramic tiles come in a wide variety of patterns and colours, are very water resistant so long as they have a good glaze and are well grouted, but the grout tends to wear and discolour in time and food can get lodged in joints and make the surface difficult to wipe clean. Marble, granite and slate are all naturally porous and need to be well polished to shrug off stains and water. They look good though and provided they are looked after will wear well.

The popular choice for wooden worktops is teak or iroko which are both hardwoods so will wear well and are waterproof once treated. In today's greener world, however, hardwoods are less frequently used unless taken from a renewable source. Despite suppliers' claims, you can never be sure of this. Soft woods like pine or beech are perfectly acceptable so long as they are well varnished, which means at least four to five coats.

This kitchen area is minute, so careful planning was vital to make good use of it. Utensils hang on racks as there aren't any drawers, a two-ring gas hob is inset in the worktop along with a small circular sink and even the stacking pans are space-saving.

Another option for finishing a worktop is Corian — a manmade material of resin and reconstituted marble. It has become very popular with architects and specifiers for its wearability and waterproof qualities when moulded into sinks and worksurfaces. The advantages are that provided it is well fitted, any joins are undetectable and so food and water don't get trapped, and it appears to be one solid piece. The drawback is its cost.

COOKING

A built-in hob is probably preferable to wasting space on a full sized cooker. Two-ring gas and electric hobs are available which can be built into a worktop. By combining a mini hob with a combination microwave, you should be able to cook most things as easily as you would with a full-sized oven except perhaps for a large joint of meat.

With only two rings you need to be a fairly well organized cook. Stacking pans will allow you to cook a whole meal on just one ring — a casserole at the bottom, potatoes on the next level and vegetables which need only a few minutes light steaming can be added at the last minute in the top level. A pressure cooker will perform the same job but in half the time and both these cooking aids are easier to store than a set of saucepans.

OTHER APPLIANCES

Once you have sorted out your cooking arrangements, there will be several other appliances to find room for — see Chapter 4 Technology Goes Tiny, for a full run down.

A fridge is a must and there are plenty of slimline models available which will fit into a run of standard base units. A washing machine, however, is probably out — the kitchen space in most studio flats just won't stretch to accommodate it. But you may find that you have room for a machine in a separate showeroom or bathroom. If you can find the space for one machine buy a combined washer/dryer — there's not much point in having somewhere to wash clothes if you have to drape them on your already limited number of radiators to dry them.

One last item which is an absolute must is a cooker hood or extractor fan over your cooking area. When you've woken up to the smell of lamb chops three mornings running you'll begin to get the point.

Bathroom

At the very least a studio flat usually has a separate bathroom or shower room. If not, you will need to select a place to site it and you will probably be limited to having a shower room as a bath will occupy too much space. You needn't see this as a disadvantage, however — there are many different types of both showers and cubicles on the market so you should get something to suit your situation. Apparently, we are becoming a nation of showerers rather than bathers — it is after all a more hygienic and greener way of keeping ourselves clean.

Before siting a shower in a flat you will need to check whether there is sufficient water pressure. Seek advice from a plumber before you put any plans into operation.

If you choose a pre-built cubicle, sliding or bi-fold doors are preferable to a pivot door as they require much less space for opening. An alternative is a fully-tiled, walk-in shower room, where you can have a basin, loo and shower in one corner of the flat. You must be absolutely sure, as indeed you should with all showers, that the areas directly around the shower are grouted and sealed perfectly to avoid any chance of leakages. The occupant of the flat below will probably not wish to share the shower — particularly if it's in his/her sitting room.

A good sofa-bed or — as shown here a convertible chaise longue — is vital for one-room living. Not only must it be comfortable, but as probably the largest item in the room it should look good too.

Living room/bedroom

We combine these two because that is exactly what you will have to do. The place where you eat, read, watch TV by day, will also be where you sleep at night. As such it needs to be pretty adaptable.

The main decision to make is what will you sleep on. The obvious choice is a sofa- or chair-bed, depending on whether you want double or single sleeping space. This item of furniture will sort out both your sleeping and seating arrangements. Alternatively, you could choose a futon, or if you really can't be bothered with all the unfolding that goes hand in hand with both these suggestions, another option is a daybed. A large divan pushed against a wall can be covered with a quilt or rug and piled with square and bolster pillows

— this will provide a comfy sofa during the day and all you have to do at night is rearrange the pillows, throw a duvet on top and your bed is made. A divan with a storage drawer underneath will give you somewhere to keep the duvet during the day.

Your living space will also need a dining area of some kind. You may have room for a largish table which will seat four to six if you have guests and which can otherwise double up as a desk. Alternatively, a table which converts from coffee table to dining table height is another idea or if you are really short on space, a dining table with flaps on either side so that you can extend it, will take up very little space most of the time.

Finding storage space is the flat dweller's nightmare but it is vital if you are to keep the place looking tidy. Make use of every possible space for built-in cupboards. Custom-made to suit any awkward shapes, they will feel more a part of the room and can be painted the same colour as the walls for camouflage.

Decorative details

The colours you choose are largely a matter of personal taste. For example, if you have an eclectic nature you may

Necessity is the mother of invention and in this studio flat, clever ideas abound. Doors are painted to blend with the background, chairs are hung on the wall and the TV and stereo are set into a false pillar which divides the kitchen from the sitting area.

want to paint walls cream or white to provide a background for decorative possessions. If you like your surroundings to be more minimal, then you can make more of walls, windows and flooring by introducing stronger colour and areas of pattern. But the key to success is continuity. When your whole home consists of just one or two rooms, continuity of colour and style are infinitely preferable to a mish-mash of design and pattern which will create confusing and untidy looking surroundings.

WALLS

Walls can be prepared or painted, but either way it is best to stick to a plain colour. You can introduce pattern in the form of fabrics or flooring, or better still with paintings or other decorative possessions. Whatever you choose, the background should be unfussy in order to keep the basic outlines as streamlined as possible.

If yours is a flat converted from a house there may be original architectural details such as cornicing, a fireplace or a large window with shutters, which you want to make the most of. Consider these in your planning and allow them, where possible, to be kept as a main attraction of the room. If you want to disguise doors paint them the same colour as the walls.

FLOORING

You will need to choose a flooring which serves several purposes. You will obviously want something in the bedroom and sitting area which is warm and comfortable underfoot, but in the kitchen and shower room the main criteria are that it is waterproof and easy to clean. You could use different types or colours of flooring to delineate the different areas but remember that by visually breaking up the area you will also make it appear smaller. It is probably better to run the same flooring throughout, or just make the change in the shower room where the door will cause a natural break anyway.

There are two good options for your main living and kitchen area. One is a laminated wood strip flooring which is comfortable and warm to walk on, and, so long as you aren't slopping water everywhere, will remain waterproof. The other is a vinyl or linoleum flooring. Both these choices are hardwearing, easy to keep clean and if you prefer, you can add a rug or two in your sitting area to warm it up a bit. A rug will also help to 'anchor' the pieces of furniture which stand around its edges, so delineating and separating the sitting area from the dining and cooking spaces.

WINDOWS

To keep your flat as light as possible during the day, the larger the windows the better. If your taste leans more towards the traditional you may want to have curtains and indeed with a large Victorian or Edwardian window you could do something sumptuous with swags and drapes to turn the whole thing into a real focal point. But if the windows or your space are quite small, the less fussy the treatment the better. In this case, Venetian slat blinds — they now come in a variety of slat widths and many colours and finishes including stained wood — are always a good choice. Slatted shutters are another option. They work in much the same way as slatted blinds, allowing you to adjust the amount of light coming in, and you can fold them right back onto the wall either side of the window so that the light is not obscured. Bear in mind, though, that they will then be taking up what might be valuable wall space. In this case, the

Simplicity is the key to success where space and light are limited as the window in this studio flat shows. Filmy muslin in two colours is enough to give privacy but diffuses the daylight beautifully too.

Venetian blinds, or even a roller blind, will be a better choice.

If your light source is limited to just one window it may be worth looking at other ways of letting in some more light. If you are on a top floor, for example, it may be possible to have a dormer window or skylight installed in the roof. This will give your room a quality of light which is totally different to that from a standard window and will really open up the whole interior. Alternatively, if by installing a shower room you have lost a light source from another window, you may be able to bring some of the light back into your main living area by putting in a glazed door to the shower room — etched or frosted glass is opaque so will retain privacy. Another good idea that we have seen is a row of 'porthole' windows along a dividing wall. Positioned quite high up on the wall they don't use up valuable wall space and also become a feature of the room.

LIGHTING

The studio flat is no exception to any other kind of home, in that well-planned lighting can go a long way to making it look just as good — or even better — at night than it does during the day. Recessed ceiling spots are a good choice for your overall lighting as they are fairly unobstrusive and can be angled to emphasize some areas and draw the eye away from others. It's an idea to have the circuit on dimmers, although make sure each area is wired to a different switch so that you can change the emphasis from one area to another if you wish.

You could supplement this general lighting with a couple of decorative table lamps in the seating area which will give you pools of light and help to separate it from the other areas of the flat when required.

CASE STUDY

This studio was a corner site with a floor area of 4.3 x 3.7m (14 x 12 ft) and a limited supply of light which has been turned into a bright, attractive studio including a shower room and a kitchen area. It is equipped with a whole range of clever ideas.

PRACTICAL POINTERS

The main living area incorporates room for both dining and sitting, with a sofa doubling as the bed and spare dining chairs hung on the wall. When not needed for dining, the black ash table can be moved nearer the sofa and lowered to coffee table height.

A hollow pillar was created to divide the kitchen and storage area from the rest of the room, and to provide built-in facilities for a television and stereo system.

The compact kitchen includes a fold-down, wall-mounted table, large enough for an individual breakfast setting, and a circular sink and two-ring gas hob are set into base units which also hide a miniature fridge. Wall-mounted racks suspend kitchen utensils within easy reach, compensating for the small area of work surface, and a clever choice of cookware — such as the stacking pans — means that it is possible to cook several items at once.

A small shower room leads off to the left, with porthole windows allowing extra light to filter through into the main room.

DECORATIVE DETAILS

One of the drawbacks of the flat was its lack of light. A slatted blind allows light in at all times but still retains privacy and a series of 'portholes' allow light to filter through from the shower room into the living area. Recessed downlights give extra light when necessary.

The shower room and cupboard doors fade into the background by being painted the same colour as the walls, and large, overhead cupboards remain unobtrusive while providing valuable extra storage space.

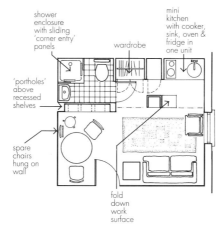

shower enclosure with sliding 'corner entry' panels

wardrobe

mini kitchen with cooker, sink, oven & fridge in one unit

'portholes' above recessed shelves

spare chairs hung on wall

fold down work surface

AT A GLANCE

• This neat studio flat incorporates kitchen, shower room and combined dining/living/sleeping space.

• The compact kitchen area includes a two-ring hob, a circular stainless steel sink and a mini-fridge, concealed behind a base-unit door.

• Integrating the television and stereo system into a pillar saves valuable surface space.

• A circular dining table seats four comfortably, six at a push. At the touch of a concealed lever it lowers to coffee table height.

• The two-seater sofa converts easily into a double bed.

• A fold-down, wall-mounted table is large enough for an individual breakfast setting.

• Shower room and cupboard doors become less noticeable when painted the same colour as the walls.

Index

Page numbers in *italic* refer to the illustrations

Acknowledgements

Key HB: *House Beautiful*

Page 7 Peter Anderson/HB; 9 Brian North/HB; 10 Roy Smith/HB; 12 Ian Parry/HB; 13 Galleried room by Hayloft Woodwork, photograph: Spike Powell/HB; 14 Brian North/HB; 16 Steve Hawkins/HB; 17 Roy Smith/HB; 19 Spike Powell/HB; 21 Range of lighting from Mazda; 22/23 Spike Powell/HB; 25 Ian Kalinowski/HB; 29 Crown Paints; 31 James Merrell/HB; 33 Textured glass by Pilkington; 34/35 Ian Parry/HB; 36 Black Ash shelving from the Inspiration range by Spur Shelving; 37 Trevor Richards/HB; 38 Fold-out ironing board and kitchen from MFI; 39 Kitchen storage system from Addis; 40 Floral bedroom storage by Lakeland Plastics; 41 Bedroom organiser system from Wickes; 43 Dennis Stone/HB; 44/45 The Micro Kitchen by Paula Rosa and Zanussi; 47 The Micro Kitchen by Paula Rosa and Zanussi, 50/51 Compact fridge, freezer and dishwasher by Electrolux; 52 ETP 200/300 mini TVs by Epson; 54/55 Study bed by Relyon; 57 Butterfly dining set from Freemans; 58 Channel 5 TV Table by Cover Up Designs; 60 Filoseat by Belinda Coote; 62 Twin Studio Storabed by Relyon; 63 Graham Rae/HB; 64/65 Peter Anderson/HB; 67 Spike Powell/HB; 69 Trevor Richards/HB; 70/71 Tom Leighton/HB; 72 Tom Leighton/HB; 73 Tony Timmington/HB; 75 Spike Powell/HB; 76 Robin Anderson/HB; 80/81 Tony Timmington/HB; 83 Tony Timmington/HB; 84 Ian Parry/HB; 85 Ian Parry/HB, detail: kitchen from the Newcastle Furniture Company; 86/87 Ian Parry/HB; 89 The Convert-A-Room System from Strachan; 91 Trevor Richards/HB; 92 Tom Leighton/HB; 94/95 Graham Rae/HB; 97 Roy Smith/HB; 99 Bath from CP Hart, photograph: Graham Seagar/HB; 100 Tribune Pentagon Shower screen and Coniston Shower tray by Armitage Shanks; 102/103 Graham Seagar/HB; 105 'Versaille' range of co-ordinated wallcoverings by Shand Kydd, photograph: Steve Dalton/HB; 106 Ian Kalinowski/HB; 107 'Graffix' range of co-ordinated wallcoverings by Crown, photograph: Steve Dalton/HB; 109 'Chablis' wallcoverings by Shand Kydd, photograph: Steve Dalton/HB; 110/111 Brian North/HB; 112 Graham Goldwater/HB; 113 Trevor Richards/HB; 116/117 Trevor Richards/HB; 119 Spike Powell/HB; 120/121 Crown paints; 124/125 Tom Leighton/HB; 127 Geoffrey Frosh/HB; 129 Galleried room by Hayloft Woodwork, photograph: Spike Powell/HB; 130/131 Geoffrey Frosh/HB; 133 Geoffrey Frosh/HB; 135 Geoffrey Frosh/HB; 136 Geoffrey Frosh/HB; 138 Trevor Richards/HB; 140/141 Geoffrey Frosh/HB.